ASPARŚA-YOGA

ASPARŚA-YOGA

A Study of Gauḍapāda's Māṇḍūkya Kārikā

COLIN A. COLE

MOTILAL BANARSIDASS PUBLISHERS
PRIVATE LIMITED • DELHI

First Edition: Delhi, 1982
Reprint: Delhi, 2004

ISBN: 81-208-1992-6

Also available at:
MOTILAL BANARSIDASS
41 U.A. Bungalow Road, Jawahar Nagar, Delhi 110 007
8 Mahalaxmi Chamber, 22 Bhulabhai Desai Road, Mumbai 400 026
236, 9th Main III Block, Jayanagar, Bangalore 560 011
120 Royapettah High Road, Mylapore, Chennai 600 004
Sanas Plaza, 1302 Baji Rao Road, Pune 411 002
8 Camac Street, Kolkata 700 017
Ashok Rajpath, Patna 800 004
Chowk, Varanasi 221 001

Printed in India
BY JAINENDRA PRAKASH JAIN AT SHRI JAINENDRA PRESS,
A-45 NARAINA, PHASE-I, NEW DELHI 110 028
AND PUBLISHED BY NARENDRA PRAKASH JAIN FOR
MOTILAL BANARSIDASS PUBLISHERS PRIVATE LIMITED,
BUNGALOW ROAD, DELHI 110 007

CONTENTS

PREFACE

This book is dedicated and offered to those individuals who intellectually and spiritually seek to understand and to penetrate the wisdom of the ancient Indian masters and seers. Just as there is once again within some sectors of the Indian population, there is a growing interest in the Western hemisphere in the yogic and esoteric disciplines of transformation, enlightenment, or self-realization. Althougth this book was penned as a Masters Thesis for the University of British Columbia in Vancouver B.C. Canada, the purpose of its writing was more than a scholastic endeavour. The present writer is interested in both the theoretical and the practical side of Indian spirituality. As the title indicates, the purpose of the present study is to explore the religio-spiritual dimension of this subject.

My effort and desire was thus to be academic and scholarly in detail and approach, while maintaining the readability of the work and its usefulness as a tool to further explore this great text, the *Māṇḍūkya Kārikā* of Gauḍapāda, by the educated and the interested lay person. It is designed for reading as it stands, especially chapters 5 and 6, or for use with the actual text in reference to the footnotes. For the individual who wishes to study the text in depth, it is advised that he read the original before, during and after reading this look, in other words, to work integrating both sources, as the text is very deep and profound and understanding emerges through interaction over time with this sort of material.

The text itself teaches a very lofty form of Non-dualism in the tradition of Advaita Vedānta and as such is unapproachable by many interested individuals. Even those familiar with Vedānta and the erudite truths of Advaita are over-whelmed by this particular text. For these reasons it is held in such high regard, and thus the study and absorption of the material is of some difficulty. This is another reason for my attempt at writing a logical and lucid account. Most of the sources are terse and without commentary, those with commentary and notes are not a step-by-step integrated account of the important religious and spiritual teachings of this marvellous text. The strictly academic themes deal with dates, style, linguistic problems, origin of ideas, philosophy, and so forth, but seldom outline the use of the text within the living tradition of spiritual knowledge which still continues in India today and wherein this *Kārikā* has an esteemed position of pre-eminence.

I would like to acknowledge the living tradition of transmission from preceptor to disciple within Advaita Vedānta, the aid of many books by religious people and scholars, the verbal account of personal contacts with knowledgeable individuals here in India, and the invaluable guidance and criticism of my professors at the University.

Colin A. Cole

ABBREVIATIONS

Bṛh. Up.	Bṛhadāraṇyakopaniṣad.
BS	Brahma Sūtra.
Ch. Up.	Chāndogyopaniṣad.
G	Śrīmad Bhagavadgītā.
MK	Māṇḍūkya Kārikā.
MUp.	Māṇḍūkyopaniṣad.
PUp.	Praśnopaniṣad.
ŚB	Śāṅkara Bhāṣya (on Brahma Sūtra).
SMV	Śārīraka-mīmāṃsā-bhāṣya-vārttika
Taitt. Up.	Taittirīyopaniṣad.

INTRODUCTION

It is alleged that Advaita Vedānta can be studied either as a system of philosophy or as a religious discipline. It is usually presented academically as a systematic metaphysic which has a religious underpinning. Little interest has been shown in its practical religious or spiritual side beyond a relatively cursory overview. Nor has the contention been elaborated beyond being merely assumed, that in Advaita Vedānta philosophy and religion are one and the same.

The present work attempts to look at these issues. The purpose of this work is to investigate the nature of the soteriology[1] of Advaita Vedānta. As this system has been heterogeneous in its expressions throughout its history, the present enquiry restricts itself to a specific author, Gauḍapāda, and his text entitled the *Māṇḍūkya Kārikā*. The author and the text have been previously analyzed and interpreted by scholars from metaphysical or philosophical perspectives or from the position which the author and the text have held in the Buddhist-Hindu philosophical interaction. Both approaches have eclipsed the religio-spiritual dimension of the text through which it has remained a part of the living tradition of Advaita philosophy and practice. Thus it has been considered necessary here to describe, analyze and

---

1. The precedent for using the term "soteriology" in the sphere of Eastern thought thus enlarging its meaning from that of "salvation" in the Western faiths to its wider use within the "liberation" oriented religions, has been established by Mircea Eliade in *Yoga : Immortality and Freedom* (Princeton University Press, 1958) and by F. J. Streng in his *Emptiness : A Study in Religious Meaning* (Nashville : Abingdon Press, 1967). Salvation, liberation, freedom, release, or however it is explained and by whatever means it is achieved is a religious task and goal. On the level of comparative or world religions, although there are many differences evident, these principles can be brought under the heading of the single concept of "soteriology". Thus it is used here in connection with Gauḍapāda's text.

interpret the religious or spiritual dimension of the text on both its theoretical and practical levels.

The study involves the problem of the inter-dependence of philosophy and religion in Advaita. Advaita is usually presented as a religious philosophy documented from the metaphysical speculation presented in a text. Seldom is Advaita regarded as a religious or spiritual pursuit wherein the philosophy is presented as a rational attempt to understand and explain this experiential dimension. Further, most studies omit, or at least appear to ignore, even the pragmatic religious material which is presented in the texts.

Gauḍapāda and his *Māṇḍūkya Kārikā* will be presented from a soteriological perspective and an emphasis will be placed on the religious versus the purely philosophical aspects of the text. This latter material has been schematically presented elsewhere. The text, then, will be looked at as a predominantly religious one and the content presented and interpreted in this light.

Chapter I-IV delineate much of the existing research in this new perspective along with new data and insights. Chapter I deals with Gauḍapāda as a religious preceptor rather than as merely a logician, metaphysician or philosopher. Chapter II examines the nature of the text, its form and purpose, and adds some further reasons for viewing it from the religious perspective as well as the philosophical. Chapter III analyzes the text for its stylistic elements which includes an inquiry into the relationship of philosophy and religion and indicates some of the teaching methods and techniques utilized. In Chapter IV a summation of Gauḍapāda's philosophy is outlined with the additional purpose of indicating the soteriological concern inherent within the metaphysics.

The remaining chapters deal with the material of Gauḍapāda's *Māṇḍūkya Kārikā* in new ways and present a description, analysis and interpretation of the religious theory and practice. Chapter V indicates the blending of philosophy and religion in the meta-psychology of the text which is the foundation of the meditative discipline elaborated by Gauḍapāda. This is followed in Chapter VI by a detailed description of the actual practices advocated in the *Kārikā* and a discussion of the results which are said to accrue from them. The final Chapter, Chapter VII, is a summary conclusion which indicates the synthetic unity of the religious and philosophical perspectives when seen from the soteriological concern of the text.

Chapter I

GAUḌAPĀDA AS PHILOSOPHER AND PRECEPTOR

I prostrate to the feet of that Great Teacher, the most adored among the adorable, who—out of sheer compassion for the beings drowned in the deep ocean of the world, infested with the terrible sharks of incessant births (and deaths)—rescued, for the benefit of all, this nectar, hardly obtainable even by the gods, from the innermost depths of the ocean of the Vedas by churning it with the (churning) rod of his illumined reason.

—from the Concluding Salutation by Śaṅkara[1]

Gauḍapāda, the author of the *Māṇḍūkya Kārikā*, was a preceptor in the tradition known today as Advaita Vedānta. In this chapter relevant background material concerning Gauḍapāda and his relation to the religio-philosophical traditions of his day will be introduced.

1. The Place of Gauḍapāda in the Tradition of Advaita Vedānta

The tradition of Advaita Vedānta had its formal philosophical and institutional beginnings with the teacher Śaṅkara, who lived circa 788-820 A.D.[2] Through his voluminous writings of both a

1. *The Māṇḍūkyopaniṣad with Gauḍapāda's Kārikā and Śaṅkara's Commentary*, translated and annotated by Swāmī Nikhilānanda, (Mysore : Sri Ramakrishna Ashrama, 1955), p. 314.

2. The date of Śaṅkara is still uncertain. "Our old traditions are so divergent that according to them as well as modern researchers we shall have to place Śaṅkara some time between the 6th century B.C. and the 9th century A.D., viz, 6th century B.C., 4th century B.C., and the 1st century

devotional and philosophical nature as well as through the creation of the *daśanāmi* orders of *sannyāsins* throughout the Indian subcontinent, Śaṅkara established what has come to be called the tradition of Advaita Vedānta. It is within the *Uttara Mīmāṃsā*, the religious philosophy based on the latter portions of the Vedic literature, the Upaniṣads in particular.

Śaṅkara acknowledges that this spiritual and philosophical heritage comes from the advaitic teachings transmitted through a succession of *gurus*. The tradition maintains that this lineage has been continuously upheld in some form since the time of the compilation of the advaitic spiritual truths and insights into the Upaniṣadic literature.A type of succession list of early Advaita is given in the traditional salutation daily repeated by the followers of Śaṅkara.[1] The order follows thus : Nārāyaṇa, the lotus-born Brahmâ, Vasiṣṭha, Śakti, his son Parāśara, Vyâsa, Śuka, the great Gauḍapāda, Govinda-Yogīndra, his disciple Śaṅkarācārya, and then his four famous disciples Padmapāda, Hastâmalaka, Troṭaka and Vārttikakāra (Sureśvara).

The first preceptor is Lord Nārāyaṇa himself and the line of succession up to Śuka is from father to son (*pitṛ-putra* or *vaṃśarṣi-paramparā*). These figures are probably mythical persons. From Śuka onwards there is the teacher-disciple succession (*guru-śiṣya* or *śiṣya-paramparā*). With Gauḍapāda commences the *mānava-sampradāya*, the traditional handing down of instruction by human agents. Gauḍapāda is the first human preceptor accorded the highest respect in the tradition. He is the first teacher or preceptor whose historicity is assured and it is from him onwards that the tradition is visible historically. Whether or not in fact Gauḍapāda was the first preceptor of

B.C., 4th century A.D., 6th century A.D., and the 9th century (788-820) A. D. The last date is now acccepted by many a scholar." V. Bhattacharya (ed., trans., and annotated), The *Āgamaśāstra of Gauḍapāda* (Calcutta : University of Calcutta, 1943), p. lxxix, fn. 8.

1. R.D. Karmarkar (ed., trans., and notes), *Gauḍapāda-Kārikā*, Poona: Bhandarkar Oriental Institute, 1953, p. i; T.M.P. Mahadevan, *Gauḍapāda : A Study in Early Advaita* (2nd ed.), Madras : University of Madras, 1952, p. 2. This succession is said to be very ancient as even Śuka is said to have lived about 3000 B.C. as he was the son of Vyāsa who lived at the time of the Mahābhārata battle.

Advaita Vedānta and that the whole tradition began with him or that he merely represents the first visible manifestation of a concrete tradition remains a conjecture. All that needs be pointed out here is that Gauḍapāda is accorded a unique position within the historical tradition on the basis of his *Māṇḍūkya Kārikā*.

Tradition regards Gauḍapāda as Śaṅkara's *paramaguru* which suggests that he was either Śaṅkara's "teacher's teacher" or that Śaṅkara regarded him as the "supreme preceptor".[1] Either way Śaṅkara accords him the highest respect and homage. Besides the mentioning of his own *guru's* name, he praises Gauḍapāda in some of his commentaries, quotes several verses from the *Kārikā* in his *Brahmasūtrabhāṣya* and perhaps of greater import, he wrote a commentary on Gauḍapāda's *Māṇḍūkya Kārikā*.[2] The very fact that Śaṅkara considered it either necessary or fruitful to write a commentary on the *Māṇḍūkya Kārikā* indicates the importance and value of this treatise of Gauḍapāda's to Advaita philosophy and practice.

Besides the continued use of the *Māṇḍūkya Kārikā* in the tradition up to this day, there is acknowledgement of Gauḍapāda and the *Kārikā* in the authoritative literature. Some references to well-known Advaitins are pertinent here. Sureśvara, an immediate disciple of Śaṅkara, quotes two *kārikās* (I. 11 and 15) in his *Naiṣkarmyasiddhi* (IV. 41 and 42) attributing them to the *Gauḍas* and this is further identified by the commentator Jñānottama as *gauḍapādīyavākyas*. This is a direct reference to a teacher Gauḍapāda. In his *Bṛhadāraṇyakopaniṣad bhāṣya-vārttika*, Sureśvara explicitly mentions Gauḍapāda by name several

1. This can account for the problem in dating. For if Gauḍapāda was indeed Govinda's *guru* that would place him during the eighth century A.D. But if the other interpretation holds true Gauḍapāda could have lived much earlier. For more details see below section 3.

2. There is a reference to Gauḍapāda in Śaṅkara's commentary on the *Śvetāśvatara Upaniṣad* (1, 8 : "*tathā ca śukaśiṣyo gauḍapādācāryaḥ*"). Even if this commentary and the one on the *Kārikā* itself are not genuine works of Śaṅkara as has been suggested, the evidence of the *Brahmasūtrabhāṣya* is sufficient. Śaṅkara quoted several verses of the *Māṇḍūkya Kārikā* (I, 16 in *ŚB* 2-1-9 and III, 15 in *ŚB* 1-4-14) which he regards as expressing the view of a teacher who knows the Vedānta tradition (*vedānta-sampradāyavid*). The language used suggests deep veneration for a great teacher.

times.[1] Vidyāraṇya in his *Pañcadaśi* (II. 28 and 29) makes a direct reference to the teacher (*ācārya*) Gauḍapāda and his teachings.[2] Sadānanda in his *Vedāntasāra* uses verses from both the *Māṇḍūkyopaniṣad* (2,5,7) and the *Kārikā* (III. 44 and 45) without reference as to their origin but suggests that they are well-known. These verses are drawn from a section of instruction for the practice of meditation and as such re-affirm both the importance and use of the *Māṇḍūkya Kārikā* as a practical teaching text within the history of the tradition

These examples and others show that Gauḍapāda's work was well known to both authors and commentators within the tradition and that he was referred to in terms of respect whether or not he was mentioned specifically by name.[3]

The text is still highly regarded and used within the tradition as a manual of instruction concerning both philosophy and practice.[4]

2. The Identity of Gauḍapāda

Now that Gauḍapāda's position within the tradition of Advaita Vedānta has been established, the identity of this great philosopher and preceptor must be determined.

---

1. In I. iv. 389 he uses the words *gauḍapādīya vacas*, in II. i. 386 he refers to the teacher as Gauḍapāda, and in a third reference (IV. iv. 886) he writes of the verses of Gauḍapāda. See Mahadevan, *Ibid.*, p.6 for further details.

2. This verse is particularly of interest here as it is a reference to, as well as a partial quote, of *MK* III. 39 concerning *Asparśa-yoga.*

3. Some other lesser known examples are as follows : Maṇḍana-Miśra quotes verses in his *Brahmasiddhi*, Ānandānubhava in chapter 4 of his *Nyāya Ratna Dīpāvali* quotes *MK* II. 32, Niscala Dāsa quotes the same verse along with other authorities in verses 322 to 341 of his *Vicāra Sāgara*, and *MK* IV. 81 and others are referred to in verses 1-13 of Sureśvara's gloss on *Mānasollāsam.* From Swāmī Rāmānanda Tīrtha, *A Writer's Study of Śaṅkara versus the Six Preceptors of Advaita* (Madras : Tinniyam Śaṅkara Mutt Bhakta Jana Sabha, 1970), pp. 15, 16, 43 and 125 respectively. The author of this work acknowledges in his introduction that his *guru* gave him the *Māṇḍūkya Kārikā* to use as a practical instruction manual.

4. For references see: *Ibid.*; and Swāmī Nikhilānanda (trans. and annotated), *The Māṇḍūkyopaniṣad with Gauḍapāda's Kārikā and Śaṅkara's Commentary.* (Mysore: Sri Ramakrishna Ashrama, 1955), pp. ii—iv and xxxiv; and others. The current use of and respect for the text was witnessed by the present writer while travelling in India during the summer of 1973.

Like most of the classical Indian textual authors, Gauḍapāda[1] is known solely through his work and the reputation handed down within his tradition. Thus traditional hagiography and his own philosophy are his only biography.[2]

That he lived and taught is evidenced by his written work, the succession of teachers claiming his lineage, and the homage paid to him within the tradition. But of the details of his life little is known except legend and some speculation.

The hagiography available helps to create an account of Gauḍapāda. Ānandagiri, in his gloss (*ṭikā*) on the *Māṇḍūkya Kārikā-Bhāṣya* IV. 1,[3] tells us that the teacher Gauḍapāda spent his time doing penance (*tapasyā*) at Badarikāśrama, the holy residence of Nara-Nārāyaṇa. It was while Gauḍapāda was in deep meditation, the legend says, that the pleased Lord Nārāyaṇa revealed the Advaita wisdom to him.[4]

The hagiographic accounts highlight two basic characteristics attributed to Gauḍapāda. These concern his practice of meditation as a part of his own pursuit of *Brahma-vidyā* and his deftness as a philosopher while being a spiritual preceptor. For example, in his commentary to Sadāśivabrahmendra's *Jagadgururatnamālāstava* Ātmabodhendra gives more information on Gauḍapāda. He says that Gauḍapāda at one time was in quest of the Self (*ātman*) under the guidance of his preceptor Śuka on a peak in

1. Traditionally he has the well-known name of Gauḍapāda. Sometimes he is called Gauḍacaraṇa (in *Śārīraka-mīmāṃsābhāṣyavārtlika* II. 9-12), Gauḍapādācārya (Śaṅkara on the *Śvetāśvataropaniṣad* I, 8), Gauḍācārya (*Pañcadaśī* II. 23) (Sāyaṇa on *Taittirīya Āraṇyaka* VII. 2), or simply Gauḍa (*Naiṣkarmyasiddhi* IV. 44) (*SMV* II. 9-12). From Bhattacharya, *op. cit.*, p. lxiv.

2. Biography, as indeed history, in India is difficult to ascertain. Hagiography is of assistance to some extent but is often of limited value. An analysis of a philosophical work is another way and may be more fruitful. See below section 5.

3. *Māṇḍūkyopaniṣad with Gauḍapāda's Kārikā, Śaṅkara's Bhāṣya and Ānandagiri's Tīkā*, Ānandāśrama Sanskrit Series 10, pp. 2 and 157.

4. Mahadevan, *op. cit.*, pp. 8-9: "That Gauḍapāda was absorbed in deep meditation most of the time we learn both from Ānandagiri and Bālakṛṣṇānanda. It is likely that the Ācarya visited Badarikāśrama and, there, was blessed with the intuitive wisdom of the Absolute. Then he must have taught those who gathered round him the truth he had discovered and embodied it in a work which came to be called the *Āgamaśāstra* or *Gauḍapādakārikā*."

the Himālayas. It was here that through Gauḍapāda's influence the erroneous views of a Buddhist teacher and his disciples were made to disappear.[1]

Bālakṛṣṇānanda (circa 17th century A.D.) in his *Śārīrakamīmāṁsābhāṣyavārttika* (II. 9-12) writes that there was in the country of Kurukṣetra a river called Hirarāvatī, on whose banks lived some Gauḍa people. Pre-eminent among them was Gauḍapāda who was absorbed in deep meditation (*samādhi*) beginning from the *Dvāpara* age and because of this his proper name is not known to those of this present age of *Kali*, though he is celebrated by the class-name of the Gauḍas.[2]

This account suggests two possibilities. It has been suggested that the designation "Gauḍapāda" is not a proper name but that this individual renounced his given name when he became a *sannyāsin*, a renunciate or an ascetic, and was eventually given this name. Another suggestion is that from the indication of his coming from Gauḍadeśa, the land of the Gauḍas (modern North Bengal), it is entirely possible that as a renunciate or as a teacher living in another part of the country, the local people called him after the name of his native place. Further, the *pāda* ending is probably an honorific title of respect as is often the custom.[3] Either way, it is accepted that the name or title "Gauḍapāda" was given to him in reference to his pursuit of spirituality.

1. Given with more detail in Mahadevan, *op. cit.*, p. 9 with reference to *Indian Historical Quarterly*, Vol. II (1959), pp. 415 ff.

2. Mahadevan, *op. cit.*, p. 3; Karmarkar, *op. cit.*, pp. iii and iv; Bhattacharya, *op. cit.*, pp. lxvii and lxvii.

3. Mahadevan, *op. cit.*, p. 8; A.V. Subbiah, "The Māṇḍūkyopaniṣad and Gauḍapāda," *Indian Antiquary*, Vol. 62 (1933), pp. 192-3; Karmarkar, *op .cit.*, p. iv. Here he suggests that the teacher was named Gauḍa as it refers to the area where he became famous. It should be noted that Sureśvara's *Naiṣkarmyasiddhi* evidence is indicative of support for Gauḍa as his place of birth. Further, Dr. Wallaser, in his *Der Altere Vedānta* (Heidelberg, 1910), suggests that Gauḍapāda is not the name of a man but is the designation of a school and that the *Kārikās* represent the views of the school of Advaita in Gauḍadeśa (i.e., the four *pādas* or books of the Gauḍas). For a summation and refutation of the arguements see Mahadevan, *op. cit.*, pp. 309 and Bhattacharya, *op .cit.*, pp. lxvii-lxx.

3. The Date of Gauḍapāda

As to the time when Gauḍapāda lived there is not as yet one undisputed date. Generally the tradition accepts the 8th century A.D. on the basis of Śaṅkara's statement that Gauḍapāda is his *paramaguru* and the interpretation which places him as the teacher of Śaṅkara's *guru* Govinda. Some accept the interpretation of this expression as that of "great teacher" which would place him any time prior to Śaṅkara. One such traditional account places him somewhere between 2900 B.C. and 900 B.C.[1] A *śākta* work called *Śrī Vidyārṇava* by Vidyāraṇya (circa 1100 A.D.) lists five *Ācāryas* between Gauḍapāda and Śaṅkara which would place him much nearer the accepted date for Śaṅkara.[2]

On the basis of strong evidence culled from Buddhist sources where verses are quoted which appear to be from the *Māṇḍūkya Kārikā*, the date of approximately 500 A.D. has been suggested.[3] This corroborates the evidence cited for a date near and yet earlier than Śaṅkara's.

Bhāvaviveka (circa 500-550 A. D.) in his *Tarkajvālā*, a commentary on his own *Madhyamika-hṛdaya-kārikā*, reviews the *Vedānta-darśana* and quotes passages from several Upaniṣads and four passages (VIII. 10-13) which appear to be drawn from the *Māṇḍūkya Kārikā* of Gauḍapāda.[4] Śāntarakṣita (705-762 A.D.) in his *Madhyamakālaṅkāra-kārikā*, 93, cites ten verses in his discussion of the views of the Aupaniṣadas. His disciple Kamalaśīla (8th century A.D.) in his commentary, the *Pañjikā*,

1. Karmarkar, *op. cit.*, pp. i-ii.

2. *Ibid.*, p. ii. There is some doubt concerning this as there may be a Gauḍapāda of the Śākta tradition. For the śākta works attributed to Gauḍapāda see section 4 below.

3. Mahadevan, *op. cit.*, pp. 13-15 following Bhattacharya, *op. cit.*, p. lxxvi.

4. For further details on these Buddhist writers see especially Bhattacharya, *op. cit.*, pp. lxxv-lxxviii. Most scholars have accepted this evidence as convincing yet there is some dissent. S.K. Belvalkar goes so far as to suggest the possibility of there having been an independent common source for both Bhāvaviveka and Gauḍapāda (*Vedānta Philosophy*, Poona 1929, p. 183) as the parallelism is not absolutely convincing.

calls these *kārikās* "*upaniṣat śāstra*" (authoritative treatise based on the Upaniṣadic teachings). If these three Buddhist writers were aware of the *Māṇḍūkya Kārikā*, Gauḍapāda must be placed before Bhāvaviveka and thus approximately in 500 A.D.

Less concrete evidence exists in the rather striking resemblances between some verses in the *Kārikā* and the *Laṅkāvatāra sūtra* and the works of Buddhist writers Nāgārjuna, Āryadeva and Asaṅga who lived between 200 and 400 A.D. These parallelisms strengthen the probability of Gauḍapāda's acquaintance with these writers and that he was either a contemporary or lived at a later date.[1]

In sum then, the upper limit for Gauḍapāda's date has been generally accepted as some time during the 8th century A.D. and the lower limit at around 500 A.D. with the possibility of his having lived as early as 200 A.D. This differs from the tradition which accepts the upper limit but also places him in the very distant past.

4. Works Attributed to Gauḍapāda

Besides the *Māṇḍūkya Kārikā*, Gauḍapāda is alleged to have composed several other works. There are seven attributed to the pen of Gauḍapāda, or, at least, to an author named Gauḍapāda. Of these two works are considered more likely than the others to have been written by this Gauḍapāda. The first is a *bhāṣya* or commentary on the *Sāṅkhya-Kārikā* of Īśvarakṛṣṇa.[2] The second work is a *vṛtti* or commentary on the *Uttara-gītā*, an assignment which is based on evidence of the colophon in one or two manuscripts. The other works include some small tāntric or *śākta* texts called

1. The important question of the interaction of Mahāyāna Buddhism and Hindu Advaita Vedānta is bracketed here as it is a complex issue and a another work in itself. The *Māṇḍūkya Kārikā* is approached herein as a statement of the Advaita Vedānta tradition. Gauḍapāda declares himself a Vedāntist in several places. See *MK* II. 12, 31, 35 et al.

2. Karmarkar, *op. cit.*, pp. v-vii says that he accepts the authorship attribution because of the traditional assignment. But other scholars contest such a view. For example : "Gauḍapāda, the commentator on Iśvarakrishna, cannot be the same person as the author of the *Māṇḍūkya Kārikā*; their philosophies are clearly too different." Mircea Eliade, *yoga: Immortality and Freedom* (2nd ed.; Princeton University Press, 1969), pp.369-370.

Subhagodayastuti and *Śrīvidyāraṇyasūtra*. The last three are commentaries on the *Durgāsaptaśatī*, the *Anugītā*, and on the *Nṛsiṃhottaratāpanīyopaniṣad*.[1]

That these works are composed by the author of the *Māṇḍūkya Kārikā* cannot be conclusively shown. Neither the view for, nor that against, attribution of these works is based on any stable ground. As such the *Māṇḍūkya Kārikā* alone will be used for an analysis of Gauḍapāda's soteriology.[2]

5. Gauḍapāda's Philosophy as his Biography

While hagiography gives a limited and often distorted description of an important and respected figure, it does emphasize certain features. These can be corroborated from other sources. One such source is the analysis of the individual's work. This is the use of philosophy as biography.

Gauḍapāda can claim to be the earliest systematic exponent of the Advaitic teachings. His teaching provided the firm foundation on which Śaṅkara and his successors in the Advaita tradition built their edifice of detailed and analytical exposition of Advaitic theory. These successors to a large degree only expounded, promulgated, framed and established the same truths as those enunciated by this early Advaitin through their skills of exegesis, exposition, logical reasoning, and experiential insight.

His philosophy indicates that he was a *brahma-niṣṭha*, one who is established in the direct knowledge of *Brahman*, i.e., an enlightened or self-realized man. Having known the non-dual truth of Reality he chose to teach others and as a preceptor guided aspirants in their pursuit of *Brahma-vidyā*. He used all the tools available to him—his own experience as a *sannyāsin*, his experiential realization, scriptural texts, logical reasoning, and the practical techniques of spiritual life known to him.

An analysis of his work indicates that Gauḍapāda had a bold vision of man, his nature and potentiality. He saw man bound

---

1. Works cited in Karmarkar., *op. cit.* pp. v-x. Karmarkar also accepts the *Uttaragītā-vṛtti* and the *Subhagodayastuti* as from the same pen as the *Māṇḍūkya Kārikā*.

2. Mahadevan, *op. cit.*, p. 30 : "Since nothing definite can be said regarding the authorship of these other works, we shall study the *Māṇḍūkya-kārikā* alone with a view to understand the philosophy of Gauḍapāda."

in *saṃsāra* unable to perceive his true nature as eternally blissful and free (*mokṣa*). His compassion and his intellect joined forces to teach and lead others to this liberation.

All that remains as his legacy is the *Kārikā* on the *Māṇḍūkyopaniṣad.* Herein, he sets forth the advaitic truths and the practical means to actualize them. His piercing intellect picks out examples of erroneous views for the aspirant which he refutes as well as gives the right understanding. He exhibits lucid reasoning, clear examples, a knowledge of the various religio-philosophical traditions of his day, the depths of his own scriptural tradition, and an acute insight into the nature of man and the universe. All these combine in the text to produce a masterly work in the *mokṣa-śāstra* (treatises specifically concerning liberation) tradition of Indian philosophical literature.

As he taught so he lived. Philosophy was not merely a pattern of ideas exhibited for human understanding, but was a system of precepts internal to the philosopher. Gauḍapāda taught practical philosophy. Philosophy for him was related to life and human experience. Philosophy must be affirmed by the direct intuitive experience of non-dual Reality, through knowing and seeing things as they really are. This experiential philosophy and the practical disciplines for its realization are his real legacy. The details of his personality remain virtually unknown.

In conclusion, the picture constructed of Gauḍapāda's identity is on the one hand minimal quantitatively, and yet on the other hand, exhibits greatness qualitatively. His biography is difficult to ascertain. The sources for this are the traditional hagiographical accounts, the place and the respect afforded him by his own tradition and those from outside who quote his work as an example of that tradition, as well as the impressions culled from his written work. These describe a man in pursuit of Self-realization, deep in meditation, who upon realizing the supreme truth becomes a great and respected preceptor leading others to the fullness of life through his philosophical exposition and the practical *sādhana* (spiritual discipline) he advocates. Gauḍapāda remains respected as both a brilliant philosopher and a great preceptor of the Advaita Vedānta tradition.

Chapter II

THE MĀṆḌŪKYA KĀRIKĀ OF GAUḌAPĀDA

With the word *Aum* etc., begins the treatise, consisting of four chapters, the quintessence of the substance of this import of Vedānta. Hence no separate mention is made of the (mutual) relationship, the subject-matter and the object to be attained. . . .This treatise must be said to contain a subject-matter on account of its revealing the means (for the realization of *Ātman*) that serves the purpose, or the end to be attained. . . This realization of non-duality is the end to be attained. This treatise is begun for the purpose of revealing *Brahman* inasmuch as by knowledge (*vidyā*) the illusion of duality, caused by ignorance, is destroyed.

—Śaṅkara's introduction to the commentary.[1]

The *Māṇḍūkya Kārikā* is the only written work of which Gauḍapāda's authorship is assured. This chapter will examine the nature of the text, its form and purpose, and give a summary overview of the work as a whole.

1. The Māṇḍūkya Kārikā

The work under discussion here is popularly known as the *Māṇḍūkya-kārikā* (or *Kārikās*). It is also known by the names *Gauḍapāda*-or *Gauḍapādīya-kārikās* and *Āgamaśāstra*.[2] These titles give us a description of the type and content of the text.

1. Swāmī Nikhilānanda, *op. cit.*, p.2.

2. Bhattacharya, *op. cit.*, p. lxi, points out different readings in different manuscripts such as, *Āgamagrantha*, *Upadeśagrantha*, *Māṇḍūkya-vārttika*, *Māṇḍūkyopaniṣad-gauḍapāda-vyākhyāna*, *Māṇḍūkyaśākhā*, or simply *Gauḍapādīya* after its author. For details on manuscripts see : Bhattacharya, *op. cit.*, pp. ix-xv (18 listed); Ānandāśrama Sanskrit Series, no. 10 edition (13 listed); Karmarkar,

The *kārikās* or verses are composed by the preceptor Gauḍapāda and represent his commentary and exposition upon ideas suggested by the *Māṇḍūkyopaniṣad*. The title *Āgamaśāstra* suggests that this text is a religious or philosophical authoritative treatise (*śāstra*) based on or concerning a scriptural teaching or doctrine handed down and established by tradition (*āgama*).

---

op. cit., p. 1 lists two more and notes, "Fortunately as regards the text of the *kārikās*, there is no difference of opinion. Professor Bhattacharya has collated a large number of Mss, but his text does not materially differ from that published in the Ānandāśrama series more than fifty years ago . . . It may therefore be taken for granted that the text of the *Kārikās* is more or less fixed."

Texts and commentaries : There are two accepted scholarly publications of the manuscripts of the *Māṇḍūkyopaniṣad* and Gauḍapāda's *Kārikā* with commentaries. They are the Memorial Edition, Vol. 5 of the *Māṇḍūkyopaniṣad* with Gauḍapāda's *Kārikā* and Śaṅkara's *Bhāṣya* and the standard Ānandāśrama Sanskrit Series, No. 10 which includes Ānandagiri's *Ṭīkā* as well. Other later commentaries exist but have not been referred to herein. For further details see Karl H. Potter, ed., *The Encyclopaedia of Indian Philosophies*, Vol. I *Bibliography* (Delhi : Motilal Banarsidass, 1970), pp.71ff. It should be noted that there are alternative interpretations by Kūranārayaṇa, Madhva and Puruṣottama for the Viśiṣṭādvaita, Dvaita and Śuddhādvaita traditions respectively in their commentaries on the *Māṇḍūkyāupaniṣad*. There are several translations of the text available. The first English translation was done in 1894 by Manilal N. Dvivedi of the *Māṇḍūkyopaniṣad with Gauḍapāda's Kārikā and the Bhāṣya of Śaṅkara* (The Bombay Theosophical Publication Fund).

This was soon followed by a German translation by Paul Deussen in 1897 (*Sechzig Upanishad's des Veda*, Leipzig). From the years 1931-5, Dr. M. Srinivasa Rao's translation of the *Māṇḍūkyopaniṣad with Gauḍapāda's Kārikā and Śaṅkara's Commentary* appeared in the *Vedānta Kesari*, Vols. xviii-xxi, Madras, 1931-5. In 1936 Swāmī Nikhilānanda's translation with annotation of the same appeared published by Sri Ramakrishna Ashrama, Mysore. Vidhushekhara Bhattacharya published a newly edited, translated and annotated edition called the *Āgamaśāstra of Gauḍapāda* in 1943 (Calcutta : University of Calcutta Press). In part a reaction to this particular edition, R.D. Karmrakar produced a new edition of the *Gauḍapāda-Kārikā* with an English translation and notes in 1953 (Poona : Bhandarkar Oriental Research Institute). In the same year Swāmī Chinmayānanda published his *Discourses on the Māṇḍūkyopaniṣad with Gauḍapāda's Kārikā* (Madras : Cinmayānanda Publication Trust). In 1957 another translation of the Upaniṣad and *Kārikā* with Śaṅkara's commentary was included in Swāmī Gambhīrānanda's *Eight Upaniṣads*, Vol. II (Calcutta : Advaita Ashrama. 1957), pp. 173-404. There are several other editions and translations into different Indian languages. For details see Potter, *Ibid.*, pp. 71ff.

Śaṅkara himself, in his introduction to the Upaniṣadic commentary, has said that the *Māṇḍūkyopaniṣad* with the *Kārikā* embodies in itself the quintessence of the substance of the entire philosophy of Vedānta.

The text consists of four chapters or *prakaraṇas* called *Āgama-prakaraṇa*, *Vaitathya-prakaraṇa*, *Advaita-prakaraṇa*, and *Alātaśānti-prakaraṇa* successively. The entire text consists of 215 metrical verses and each chapter contains 29, 38, 48 and 100 verses respectively.

It is only the first chapter, the *Āgama-prakaraṇa*, where the *mantras* or verses of the *Māṇḍūkyopaniṣad* are expressly delineated. The remaining chapters deal with subjects related to the Upaniṣad but follow independent directions. As such, Gauḍapāda's *Kārikā* is not a commentary on the *Māṇḍūkyopaniṣad* in the usual sense of the term.

2. The Type of Text

Gauḍapāda's work is not a *bhāṣya* or commentary type of literature although several commentators refer to it as similar to a commentary. It is not a *bhāṣya* in that the form would then be like Śaṅkara's *bhāṣya* on this *kārikā*—a word by word explanation and exposition.

Although Ānandagiri calls it a *vārttika*, by definition it is not one, as a commentary of this sort is an explanatory work dealing with what is said, not said and said badly in the original work. Nor can it be a *vyākhyā* or exposition of the Upaniṣad, for it is only the first chapter which really deals with the upaniṣadic text per se.[1]

Gauḍapāda's work is a *Kārikā*, a serious treatise whose purpose is to expound in a metrical form an aspect of a subject or a particular doctrine so that it would be easy to memorize it. The object here is the same as that of the *sūtras* or aphoristic literature

1. Even here there is not a word by word commentary nor a step by step analysis of the Upaniṣad. Gauḍapāda re-arranges the ideas into a pattern which easily conveys the central point concerning *Turīya*, the Absolute non-dual Reality and passes over that which is not directly useful for his elaboration. Also, he expounds some ideas only hinted at or suggested by this compact, cryptic text.

but with some differences. While the *sūtras* are in prose and aim at condensation to an extreme degree, the *kārikās* which are metrical verses are not so brief and cryptic.

Both are related to the oral form for the purpose of memorization and both require commentary to some degree.[1] As the *sūtras* are very short and terse they need extensive commentary in order to cover an entire system. The *kārikās* are not as brief as *sūtras*, while not fully developed as the *śāstra* or treatise literature. The *kārikā* form is defined by Hemacandra as that which indicates profound meaning in a few words. The *kārikā* literature, then, ordinarily deals with a clarification of themes and expounds on an aspect or a single phase of a subject.

There are two types of Advaita manuals, the expository and the polemical. This work does not attempt to answer criticisms by opponents nor necessarily to refute the detailed arguements of other schools or thinkers. It is rather a *prakaraṇa-grantha*, a "book of categories", which is an expository text dealing with the basic ideas of the system. As a text-book of instruction it usually includes an *upadeśa* section on the practical methods and concerns of *sādhana* (spiritual discipline).

Gauḍapāda's *Māṇḍūkya Kārikā* is considered to be an *upadeśa-grantha* as is evident from the colophons in some of the manuscripts.[2] The text is a work whose main purpose is to teach those who seek to know the essentials of Advaita Vedānta and to constructively help the student understand the tenets of the tradition itself. The method adopted is the direct mode of setting forth the teachings and clarifying the ideas involved therein. The purpose of this is the spiritual welfare of the students concerned.[3] Every

1. For this reason Śaṅkara's commentary will be used discriminatively and only where it is necessary to understand difficult sections of the text. The present writer is aware of the problems of interpretation that occur with the use of a later commentary, even if it is from within the same tradition.

2. Mahadevan, *op. cit.*, p. 63. The term *upadeśa* is used by Gauḍapāda himself in I.18.

3. Mahadevan, *op. cit.*, p. 170: "The purpose of (*upadeśa-*) *śāstra* is to enable the aspirant to cross the sea of *saṃsāra* and reach the shore of blessedness which is the highest human goal." See also Śaṅkara's introductory quotation at the beginning of this chapter.

upadeśa-śāstra contains particular advice to help the *sādhaka* on the spiritual path.

Gauḍapāda's *Kārikā* is true to this two-fold character of *upadeśa-śāstra.* On the one hand, he expounds on a basic scriptural text and delineates the basic tenets of Advaita from different perspectives. And, on the other hand, he provides practical teachings at the end of each chapter in particular and also some advice throughout the text in general. Though there is an apparent two-fold division they are in fact one, for theory and practice go hand-in-hand and are reciprocally related in this tradition.

3. The Māṇḍūkyopaniṣad

The *Māṇḍūkya Kārikā* is said to be an exposition of the short but important Upaniṣad named the *Māṇḍūkya.*[1] This late Upaniṣad is considered to be one of the principal Upaniṣads by all schools of Vedānta. Although it consists of only twelve prose verses it is unique in its summation of upaniṣadic thought.

---

1. Traditionally Gauḍapāda's *Kārikā* is said to be centered around the *Māṇḍūkyopaniṣad.* Some rival traditions and some modern scholars suggest this is not so. The problems here can be grouped into three different contentions. They are as follows :

(i) The *Māṇḍūkyopaniṣad* does not consist of the 12 prose passages alone but also of the 20 *Kārikās* of the first *prakaraṇa.*

(ii) There is no Upaniṣad named the *Māṇḍūkya.* Gauḍapāda was the author of the prose passages as well as the *Kārikās* of the first *prakaraṇa.*

(iii) T.M.P. Mahadevan, *op. cit.*, reviews the arguments and deals with these contentions (pp. 32-55). On these problems he concludes that there is "no reasonable ground to reject the tradition regarding the relationship between the Upaniṣad and the first *prakaraṇa* of the *Kārikā.* The very name of the *prakaraṇa Āgama* signifies that it is based on a scriptural text" (p. 65). V. Bhattacharya, *op. cit.*, pp.xxxi-xlvii also examines the arguments of other scholars. The material on these questions are drawn from : (1) V. Bhattacharya ("The *Māṇḍūkyopaniṣad* and the *Gauḍapāda-Kārikā*," *Indian Historical Quarterly*, Vol. I [1925], pp. 119-125, 295-302), (2) B.N.K. Sarma ("Upaniṣadic theory of Gauḍapāda's *Kārikā*, "*Poona Orientalist*, Vol. 1.2 [1936-7], pp. 27-38; "Further light on *Gauḍapāda Kārikās*," *Review of Philosophy and Religion*, Vol. 3.1, pp. 45-55; "New light on the *Gauḍapāda-Kārikas*, "*Review of Philosophy and Religion*, Vol. 2.1 [1931], pp. 35-56: "Still further light on the *Gauḍapāda Kārikās*," *Review of Philosophy and Religion*, Vol. 4.2 [1933], pp. 174-195), (3) Y. Subrahmanya Sarma ("Upaniṣadic theory of the *Gauḍapāda-Kārikās*,"

Upaniṣad-brahmayogin, a commentator on the 108 Upaniṣads, characterizes the *Māṇḍūkyopaniṣad* as *sarva-vedānta-sāriṣṭha* (the essence of the entire Vedānta). The later *Muktikopaniṣad* describes it as the one Upaniṣad which alone is sufficient for the attainment of truth and liberation.[1]

This text, though brief, contains what may be considered the key passages of non-dualism. It incorporates many levels of reference in its synthesis of Upaniṣadic, yogic, mystical and cosmological elements.[2] This integration of material in only a dozen verses makes it extremely terse and subtle.

The *Māṇḍūkyopaniṣad*, like other Upaniṣads, discusses the problem of Ultimate Reality. The knowledge of *Brahman* or *Ātman* is its theme. It uses homologies based on the syllable *OM* (*AUM*) in an attempt to explain all experience. *Brahman* or *Ātman* is explained through its manifestation as the four *pādas* or quarters of the different states of experience. It tells how the *Ātman* is associated with the three states of waking, dream and deep sleep and then how these states are related to *Turīya*, the fourth, which designates Ultimate Reality.

Along with this explanation it teaches a method of meditation for the enquirer to realize this within his own experience. The subjective approach herein is one of enquiry and negation of that which is finite and limited, working from the more gross manifestations of experience and piercing progressively towards the subtler ones until the aspirant realizes that the self (*Ātman*) is *Brahman* (*ayam ātmā brahma*).[3]

Considering the *Māṇḍūkyopaniṣad's* unique place in Advaita literature it is no wonder that Gauḍapāda chose this scriptural text as the primary operational base for his exposition.

Review of Philosophy and Religion, Vol. 4.2 [1933], pp. 196-204), and (4) A.V. Subbiah ("The *Māṇḍūkyopaniṣad* and Gauḍapāda," *Indian Antiquary*, Vol. 62 [1933], pp. 181-193; "Gauḍapāda's *Āgamasāstra*," *Indian Historical Quarterly*. Vol. II, [1935], pp. 783-790; "Are *Gauḍapāda-Kārikās śruti* ?", *Poona Orientlist*, Vol. I.1 [1936], pp. 7-18, Vol. I. 2, pp. 2-12).

1. *Māṇḍūkyamekamevāla mumukṣūṇām vimuktaye.*

2. Eliade, *Yoga*, pp. 122-124.

3. *Māṇḍūkyopaniṣad* 12. This is one of the famous *Mahāvākyas* of the Vedāntic literature which also occurs in *Bṛhadāraṇyakopaniṣad*, II.5.19.

4. The Scope of the Māṇḍūkya Kārikā

The *Māṇḍūkya Kārikā* of Gauḍapāda is a work containing four chapters.[1] In this *upadeśa-śāstra* he sets forth the essentials of the Advaita Vedānta teachings concerning non-dualism.

In the first chapter, the *Āgama-prakaraṇa*, Gauḍapāda uses the *Māṇḍūkyopaniṣad* as his basic scriptural text (*śruti*) and begins with a summary of its teachings. He focuses on the analysis of the three states of experience (*avasthās*) in order to show that the Self which is referred to as the *Turīya*, the fourth, underlies and transcends the changing states of experience.

The second chapter, *Vaitathya-prakaraṇa*, deals with the idea of the illusoriness or falseness of the world of plurality. This Gauḍapāda seeks to establish and explain on the basis of various illustrations, the analogy of dreams, and through a criticism of creation theories.

The *Advaita-prakaraṇa,* the third chapter, seeks to show the non-illusoriness of non-duality. Through citations from scripture and reasoning he details the arguments for the truth of *advaita* (non-dualism). It is in this chapter that the major discussion of the path to the realization of non-duality called *Asparśa-yoga* is given.

The last chapter, called the *Alātaśānti-prakaraṇa*, repeats some of the arguements of the earlier *prakaraṇas.* It shows the unintelligibility of the concept of causality through the use of dialectical

1. There are several views concerning the inter-relation of the four *prakaraṇas*. These differing views can be summarized in three possible positions: 1. that the work is an integrated whole, 2. that each *prakaraṇa* is a separate work and the *Māṇḍūkya Kārikā* is a compilation of the four treatises, and 3. that the chapters could have been written separately and thus could be either seen as independent works or as complementary treatises which can be easily taken together. The first view is the one traditionally held particularly as Śaṅkara right at the beginning of his commentary accepts the work as an integrated whole, assumes the contiguity of the four *prakaraṇas,* and deftly argues for this inter-relation. It is also accepted by the scholars T.M.P. Mahadeven and R.D. Karmarkar. The second view is held by V. Bhattacharya. For details see *op. cit*., pp. xlvii-lvi. These are taken up by Karmarkar *op. cit.*, pp. xxiii-xli and Mahadevan, *op. cit.*, pp. 55-63. The third view is a compromise situation resulting from the weight of the arguments given on both sides. The present exposition assumes the first view with deference to the third and thus takes the work as a whole whatever the precise relationship of the four *prakaraṇas*.

reasoning which points out the mutual contradictions of the opposing or different schools of thought prominent at his time, explains and argues the illusoriness of the phenomenal world, and establishes the truth of non-duality which, Gauḍapāda proclaims, is eternally "unborn" or "unoriginated" (*ajātivāda*).

One summary of the work as a whole is that of the commentator Śaṅkara.

> The first chapter, then, seeks, by dealing specifically with the Vedic texts, to indicate the (traditional) means to the realization of the essential nature of *Ātman* and is devoted to the determination of the meaning of *Aum*. The second chapter seeks rationally to demonstrate the unreality of duality; the illusion (duality) being destroyed, the knowledge of non-duality (becomes evident), as the cessation of the imagination of snake etc., in the rope reveals the real nature of the rope. The third chapter is devoted to the rational demonstration of the truth of non-duality, lest it should, in like manner, be contended to be unreal. The fourth chapter is devoted to the rational refutation of the other schools of thought which are antagonistic to the truth as pointed out in the Vedas and which are opposed to the knowledge of the Advaitic Reality, by pointing out their falsity on account of their own mutual contradiction.[1]

This statement is made from the perspective of those who see Gauḍapāda as a systematic philosopher which indeed he was. And yet an analysis of the work clearly shows that this is to some extent merely an overview which ignores or passes lightly over much other material and also other possible uses of the same material. For Gauḍapāda was not only a great philosopher, he was also a preceptor concerned with the spiritual welfare of those to whom he taught. This aspect of the text will be explored further in the following chapters.

1. Swāmi Nikhilānanda, *op. cit.*, p. 3. This understanding of Gauḍapāda's text is reaffirmed in Śaṅkara's commentary on *MK* IV.1.

CHAPTER III

STYLISTIC ELEMENTS OF GAUḌAPĀDA'S *MĀṆḌŪKYA KĀRIKĀ*

> Diversity would disappear if it had been imagined by anyone. This kind of talk is for the sake of (making) instruction (possible). Duality ceases to exist after realization. —*MK* I.18

> The separateness of the individual and the supreme Self that has been declared (in the Vedic texts) earlier than (the talk of) creation (in the Upaniṣads), is only in a secondary sense that keeps in view a future result (viz. unity); for such separateness is out of place in its primary sense. —*MK* III. 14

> The creation that has been multifariously set forth with the help of the examples of earth, gold, sparks, etc., is merely by way of generating the idea (of oneness); but there is no multiplicity in any way. —*MK* III. 15[1]

This chapter will provide material to further indicate the importance of the soteriological nature of Gauḍapāda's teaching as embodied in the *Māṇḍūkya Kārikā*. An attempt will be made to indicate the various modes and devices which Gauḍapāda uses in his text as an aid to teaching both philosophy and practice. Two areas will be dealt with here. The nature of Advaita Vedānta will be described in terms of the juxtaposition of philosophy and religion and the relationship between these two aspects will be given in general. The stylistic elements within

1. All quotations of the *kārikās*, unless otherwise indicated, are from Swāmi Gambhirānanda's translation found in his *Eight Upaniṣads* (Calcutta : Advaita Ashrama, 1966) pp. 173-404.

the *Māṇḍūkya Kārikā* which Gauḍapāda uses to delineate these aspects of Advaita Vedānta will also be indicated.

1. The Religio-Philosophical Nature of Advaita Vedānta

Advaita Vedānta is a religio-philosophical tradition. It is one of the classical Indian *darśanas* or systems of thought. *Darśana* literally means "perspective" or "point of view" and suggests that there are different ways of understanding and answering the problems which concern religion and philosophy.[1] While there are philosophies in the literature concerning *artha* (worldly affairs), *dharma* (secular and religious duty), and *kāma* (the pleasures), and so forth, the designation of "philosophy" in India is usually reserved for the *Mokṣaśāstra* literature.

The Advaita Vedānta system of thought and practice is definitely a part of the *mokṣa* (liberation) oriented philosophies. As a *darśana* it is *āstika* or orthodox within the Brahmanical

1. The current discussion concerning the religious orientation of Indian philosophy as a whole will be omitted as it is not necessary to enter into the debate here. The problem and its intricacies are noted, but as the present work limits itself to a specific text within the tradition of Advaita Vedānta, the debate is to a large extent peripheral for this system, and especially for Gauḍapāda, as will be pointed out below. The debate revolves around the issue of the purpose of the particular "philosophy" and the emphasis given by the specific individual textual author. The tradition of Advaita Vedānta is definitely *Mokṣa* or liberation oriented and this aim is very clear in Gauḍapāda's *Kārikā*.

For details concerning this debate, see for example, S. Radhakrishnan, *Indian Philosophy*, Vol. I (London : George Allen and Unwin, 1927) pp. 24 ff, and reaction from R.H. Robinson, "Classical Indian Philosophy," in Joseph Elder, ed., *Chapters in Indian Civilization*, Vol. I (Kendall / Hunt Publishing Co. 1970), pp. 129-227. See also : Karl H. Potter, *Presuppositions of India's Philosophies* (Westport : Greenwood Press, 1963) ; Swāmi Agehānanda Bhārati, *A Functional Analysis of Indian Thought and its Social Margins* (Varanasi : Chowkhamba Sanskrit Series Office, 1964) ; Charles A. Moore, "Philosophy as distinct from religion in India," *Philosophy East and West*, Vol. XI. Nos. 1 and 2 (April—July 1961), pp. 3-26; P.T. Raju, "Religion and spiritual values in Indian thought," *Philosophy East and West* Vol. IX, Nos. 1 and 2 (April—July 1959), pp. 38-40, *The Philosophical Traditions of India* (London : George Allen and Unwin , 1971), and other works; Daya Krishna, "Three conceptions of Indian philosophy," *Philosophy East and West*, Vol. XV (1965), pp. 37-51; et al.

tradition. It is a school within the group called the *Uttaramīmāṃsā*, or more popularly, the *Vedānta*, the latter portion or end (*anta*) of the Vedic literature. Like all the *Mīmāṃsā* schools it is true to the name—a systematic enquiry or investigation of this scripture. As it bases itself on the non-dual teachings therein it is designated *advaita-vāda*.

The essential problem of Advaita Vedānta, which the tradition calls the fundamental problem of human life, is the problem of liberation (*mokṣa*). It is concerned with how human life may retain its true significance, anywhere and at anytime. This is man's natural urge to search for meaning and value in life. The necessary pre-requisite for this is the task of analyzing the human situation in comprehensive and thorough-going manner. It must enquire into and analyze the basic aspects of human affairs such as the nature of the world, knowledge, principles of human conduct, religious beliefs, and so forth.[1]

Philosophy and religion come together when it is seen that the central problems of life are centered in man. The answers to these problems or issues concerning the nature and relationship of man to the world and of both of these to ultimate Reality are reflected in the advocated behaviour and practices appropriate to this situation.[2]

---

1. "Philosophy is the attempt to think out the presuppositions of experience, to grasp, by means of reason, life or reality as a whole. It seeks to discover a rational explanation of the universe—an explanation which gives to all parts, nature, God and man, their due, views all things in their right proportion, and resolves the contradictions of experience. Philosophy has to find out an all-comprehensive and universal concept which itself requires no explanation, while it explains everything else. It must be the ultimate reality into which all else can be resolved and which cannot itself be resolved into anything else. Philosophy is the theory of reality if by reality we mean something that exists of itself and in its own right and not merely as a modification of something else. The test of a philosophic theory is its capacity to co-ordinate the wealth of apparently disconnected phenomena into an ordered whole, to comprehend and synthesise all aspects of reality." S. Radhakrishnan, *The Reign of Religion in Contemporary Philosophy* (London : MacMillian and Co., Ltd., 1920), p. 412.

2. "Philosophy is meant.. to understand what one is, what one can and ought to become in this world, how one can become it, and what the nature of the world is in which one has one's being and can attain the ideal of life. It

Advaita Vedānta is such a synthesis of theory and practice, being at once an enquiry into the nature of *Brahman* which is regarded as the highest Reality, and a search for the way to the spiritual realization of *Brahman* regarded as the supreme goal of life. Thus there are two dominant features of Advaita Vedānta, its metaphysical investigation and its consideration of the way of life to fulfil this quest. The pursuit of this two-fold orientation has produced an ontolngy, a theory of knowledge, a psychology, an ethical system, and a philosophy of religion amongst other things. The combination or rather integration of these elements into a "system," "school," or "tradition" is the sense in which Indians understand "philosophy."[1]

The unity of *Ātman-Brahman* is the aim of philosophical thought and the goal of spiritual attainment in Advaita Vedānta. Philosophy and religion blend to a large degree and yet each has its own sphere and can be treated separately, to a point, as a system of thought on the one hand, and as a path of spiritual experience on the other. The theoretical aspect concerns the desire to understand the nature of the universe and the nature and status of man therein. The practical aspect concerns the discovery of the fundamental principles of conduct and the

---

is necessary to understand both oneself and the reality in which one has one's being; for one has to know whether the nature of oneself and of reality allows the achievement of the ideal." P.T. Raju, *The Philosophical Traditions of India*, (London: George Allen and Unwin, 1971) p. 16.

1. The words "philosophy", "religion", and "spirituality" do not mean exactly the same things to the Indian and to the westerner. "Philosophy", as has been indicated, refers to a "way of life" which consists of both the elements of theory and practice. *Darśana* as view, theory, or perspective of reality, and *mata* as opinion, doctrine or theory within the *mokṣa* attitude is uniquely Indian in comparison to the usual western definition of philosophy as the love of wisdom or knowledge for its own sake. That there have been similarities throughout history is not being denied here. "Religion" in India and particularly in Advaita Vedānta is often considered to be within the realm of *dharma* and "spirituality" falls within the scope of the *mokṣa* attitude. Spirituality, in this context, is different from its western counterpart which usually relates to what is also designated as religion. In Advaita Vedānta it is a specific reference to the highest quest, the search for the Self (ātman) as the quintessence of life. "Religion" and "spirituality" are used interchangeably herein as it is more consonant for westerners although the full gamut of the Indian meanings for both terms will be referred to herein.

disciplines or techniques to be utilized for the attainment of complete human freedom. These aspects again are not really unrelated, but are of necessity mutually determining.[1]

Philosophy and religion are thus said to be interwoven and even coincide in Advaita Vedānta. Philosophy and religion are the theoretical and practical aspects of one and the same attempt at realizing the highest end of life. Philosophy forms the theoretical basis of religious or spiritual experience. It is the interpretation and rational justification of the religious experience which also supplies the practical confirmation of the theoretical doctrines of philosophy. It is the task of philosophy to try to translate and understand analytically in terms of thought or conceptual thinking what has been presented in the living experience of spiritual intuition. In the case of Advaita, it starts from experience and it recognizes experience to be the goal of philosophy.[2] Reason justifies the experiences of religion, can show the experience to be consistent, but cannot yield the experience itself which transcends reason. Philosophy cannot give us the experience but merely shows what is possible. The merely possible demands verification or an actualization in concrete experience. It is practical *sādhanā* which makes the realization of this experience possible.[3]

---

1. "In the philosophy of religion there is so close a connection between the statement of principle and the sequence of appropriate deeds that a divorce between them, other than momentary, is out of the question; religion when not backed by behaviour is held to be infertile and even unreal." Dunham, *The Religion of Philosophers*, p. 2.

2. "Advaita as philosophy aims to seek that which is discovered or realized by Advaita as religion or mysticism. As philosophy, Advaita has nothing more in it than to plan its procedure in evaluating the things of experience in this light. Its orientation, then, must be different from all other pursuits which equally discuss logic, epistemology, psychology, axiology etc. In all these modes of philosophy, the orientation of Advaita should never be lost sight of." K.B. Ramakrishna Rao, *Three Lectures on Advaita as Philosophy and Religion* (Mysore : University of Mysore, 1969), pp. 8-9.

3. While experience is said to be prior in Advaita, the following statement concerning the effect of doctrine on subsequent experience and practice is also true. "Vedāntic *sādhana* is the substantial hypostasis of which the doctrine may be considered as an attribute. The reverse too is true. For the *sādhana* that starts now is initiated and maintained by the inspiration coming

Thus in Advaita Vedānta the categories of perspectives of metaphysics, epistemology, psychology, and soteriology are interwoven and interrelated and reciprocally influence each other.[1]

To a preceptor such as Gauḍapāda there are really none of these divisions, for from his perspectives he talks only of Truth and only uses different ways to communicate this to his students to aid them in their direct realization of it. As a *guru* he is uninterested in these categories and yet as a philosopher he is aware of some necessary procedures in outlining arguments and offering clear explanations. An analysis of the text shows no real concern with these divisions. Also, the explicit division and utilization of these precise categories did not really develop within Advaita Vedānta until a later date.

In conclusion, then, Advaita Vedānta is a religion as much as it is a technical philosophy. It is a way of spiritual realization as well as a system of thought. As a philosophical system it attempts to deal with the nature of reality, aims to give a unified account of existence as a whole, and to present a schematic interpretation of the sum total of experience. Its religious orientation provides a practical guide to spiritual

---

from the already established doctrine. In consequence the spiritual experience will be inevitably determined by the metaphysics to which the *sādhaka* has already bound himself by his faith in its validity. (p.61) ". . the metaphysics of a doctrine imparts a positive direction to the spiritual endeavour. It also invests the experience with its particular content and is its ground and support throughout all its phases." (p.81). D. Prithipal, *Advaita Vedānta* (Varanasi : Bharatiya Vidya Bhavan, 1969).

1. A reasonable account can be found in Prithipal, *op. cit.*, pp.69-74. For example, he shows that "there is no demarcation sundering epistemology from metaphysics. While the entire Vedāntic doctrine serves as an indication to Being its theory of knowledge likewise acts as a handmaid to the spiritual *sādhana*, epistemology and *sādhana* operate within the fold of ignorance. The interpenetration of philosophy and experience leaves no room for a possible antagonism on the intellectual level between Vedāntic epistemology and metaphysics." (p.69) "It is no exaggeration to say that Vedānta synthesises theology, philosophy with experience (*anubhava*) so that the whole system is complete only with the participation of the practicing *sādhaka*." (p.71) It is this last aspect which is the unifying element around which the system is constructed.

experience. As such it gives advice and outlines practices conducive to release and Self-realization in correspondence to the findings of philosophical investigation.

Gauḍapāda as the earliest systematic Advaitin is true to this orientation of Advaita Vedānta. The following chapters will provide his unique contribution to Advaita as philosophy and religion.

2. The Theological Concerns of Advaita Vedānta and Gauḍapāda

> This system primarily aims at determining the purport of the Vedāntas or Upaniṣadic texts and unlike other rational systems, is not meant for establishing or refuting any particular system by means of pure ratiocination.
>
> —from Śaṅkara's *Brahma Sūtra Bhāṣya* 2.2.1

> This Highest Reality, however, has to be ascertained from the Vedāntic texts only. —Śaṃkara on *MK* IV. 99

The *Mimāṃsā darśanas* are scripturally based schools of thought. As such they are involved with exegesis and interpretation of revealed texts. In this sense the Vedāntic schools as a whole are really dealing with "religious" or "theological" philosophy rather than with "critical" philosophy.[1]

A Vedāntic system, such as Advaita, bases itself upon ancient scriptural texts, and one of its primary tasks is to show that these represent a consistent viewpoint. In this way, systematic Vedānta was formulated in terms of scriptural exegesis as much as it was formulated in terms of philosophical analysis.

Scripture (*śruti*) is one of the valid sources of knowledge (*pramāṇas*) in Indian philosophy and especially in the Vedānta schools of thought. Besides the commonly accepted instruments of knowledge like perception (*pratyakṣa*) and inference (*anumāna*), verbal or written authority (*śabda*) is accepted. In the tradition

1. Note that the term theology is not necessarily related to the concept of God, but rather to the scriptural nature of such systems. See also : Bharati, *op. cit.*, pp.104 ff; Robinson, *op. cit.*, pp. 217-8; Smart, *op. cit.*, p. 15 etc. This also suggests the point made in section 1 above concerning the inter-relation and the mutual determination of religious experience and philosophy.

of Advaita it is accorded the highest place, as in the last analysis the other *pramāṇas* are dependent on agreement with authority. More important, it is considered to be the final or only means of knowledge because it can show us what the other *pramāṇas* are incapable of disclosing. It shows the object and goal of spiritual life and thus dispels the *avidyā* or ignorance concerning *Brahman,* the Highest Reality. Thus it is said traditionally, that Advaita Vedānta begins in *śruti* and ends in *anubhūti,* direct experience of Reality.[1]

The central concern of Advaita is to establish the oneness of Reality and to lead the *sādhaka* to the realization of it. The Upaniṣads, which are literally the "end" of the *Veda* or the "crown of *śruti*", contain the spiritual discoveries made by the ancient seers (*ṛṣis*). They are considered to be a record of the experiences of these sages and are designed to initiate the aspirant into the secrets of this intuitive experience. These declarations constitute the testimony of Self-realization (*ātma-sākṣātkāra*). In this way they are held to be unique and very valuable.

The aspirant is required to place faith in these texts during his pursuit but the final test in Advaita is always experience. The goal of the enquiry into the nature of Reality (*brahma-vijñāna*) is direct personal intuitive experience (*anubhava*). Because of this, scripture is also "devalued" as having but a methodological value in the pursuit of the realization of *Brahma-vidyā*. *Śruti* as other's experience is but mediate knowledge (*parokṣa*) and only when this becomes immediate knowledge (*aparokṣa jñāna*) has scripture fulfilled its purpose. This mediate knowledge must become immediate, personal, integral experience.

Gauḍapāda as both a philosopher and a preceptor uses *śruti* in this fashion. His *Kārikā* is based on a scriptural text, the *Māṇḍūkyopaniṣad,* and is an exposition of the ideas found or suggested therein. As such he explains *śruti* as well as makes use of it in his teaching. As the possible interpretations of scripture are many, Gauḍapāda sets out to give a systematic

1. This indicates the later formal Advaita epistemology wherein *śruti* is given a high place amongst the *pramāṇas* and *anubhūti* is given the highest place.

interpretation or explanation of this from the standpoint of absolute non-dualism and as such represents the first of its kind, as far as the extant literature goes, in the tradition of Advaita Vedānta. One of the text names *Āgamaśāstra*, suggests this orientation.

As it is the philosophy of the Upaniṣads which Gauḍapāda expounds, it is natural that he should quote and make reference to these scriptures. Again, the first *prakaraṇa* is based on the *Māṇḍūkyopaniṣad*. Here and in the other chapters, Gauḍapāda makes frequent allusions to other scriptural texts.[1] The major sources for Gauḍapāda are the *Bṛhadāraṇyaka Upaniṣad* in particular, as well as the *Chāndogya*, *Kaṭha*, *Taittirīya*, *Kauṣītaki*, *Praśna* and *Īśa* Upaniṣads.[2]

When Gauḍapāda refers to a topic discussed in scripture, he uses such expressions as *prakāśita* (it has been made clear), *samprakāśita* (made very clear), and *vedānta-niścaya* (the settled conclusion arrived at in Vedānta).[3] Thus Gauḍapāda does not claim originality for his views. He employs the word *smṛta* from the root *smṛ*, "to remember," eleven times[4] which indicates that

1. For example, in II. 31 Gauḍapāda uses the term *vedānteṣu* by which he means the Upaniṣadic literature; in III. 11 there is reference to the *Madhu-Brāhmaṇa* chapter of the *Bṛhadāraṇyaka Upaniṣad*; in III. 23 Gauḍapāda uses the word *śruti* itself, in III. 24 he gives partial quotations from the *Kaṭha* (II. 1. 11), *Bṛhad. Up.* (II. 15. 19), and *Yajur Veda* (XXXI. 19); III. 25 talks of texts and gives *Bṛhad.* III. 9. 28 as reference; III. 26 refers to the famous *neti, neti* of *Bṛhad.* II. 3. 6; etc.

2. For precise details concerning the Upaniṣadic basis of the *Māṇḍūkya Kārikā* see T.M.P. Mahadevan, *op. cit.*, pp. 65-80 and Bhattacharya, op. cit., pp. lxxxx-ciii. Mahadevan concludes that, "There can be no doubt therefore, that Gauḍapāda is an *Aupaniṣada* teacher whose sole purpose in writing the *Kārikā* is to expound the central teaching of the Upaniṣads" (p. 80). Karmarkar. *op. cit.*, p. iv, adds that the *Kārikā* may be indebted to the *Bhagavad-Gītā* also. Further, he suggests that, "It is not unlikely that Gauḍapāda who seems to be indebted to the *Bhagavad-Gītā* for many ideas in his *kārikā*, may have thought of emphasising the Yoga element in the *Gītā* by writing a supplement to it" (p. ix). As to the possible source within Buddhist materials, mention has been given above.

3. *MK* II. 3 and III. 12; III. 11; and II. 12 respectively. Mahadevan, *op. cit.*, p. 89.

4. *MK* I. 1, 20, 26; II. 4, 7; III. 1; IV. 32, 46, 88, 90, 94. Bhattacharya, *op. cit.*, p. lxiii.

he refers to doctrines or teachings handed down traditionally, either from scriptural and authoritative texts or from previous teachers. This is also clear from his use of terms which suggest both self-realized beings and intelligent interpreters of scripture. He calls them *munis* (sages), *manīṣins* (the wise), *vicakṣaṇas* (subtle seers), *tattvavids* (knowers of truth), *vedapāragas* (those who have reached the other shore of the Vedas), *buddhas* (the enlightened), *vipras* (the wise), *vidvāns* (the learned), *mahādhīs* (of great intellect), and *mahājñānas* (great knowers).[1]

From all this it is clear that Gauḍapāda not only asserts his own experience but quotes and refers to the past tradition of teachers, predominantly to those of the Upaniṣadic literature. He firmly bases himself and his teaching in the scriptural tradition and from there develops his philosophy. From the truths of scripture he points out the goal of the spiritual life and the means thereto. Scripture is the highest *pramāṇa* and as mediate knowledge must be actualized in experience (*anubhava*). This use of scripture as *śravaṇa*, as "hearing," will be explained further below.

3. The Use of Reason in Advaita Vedānta and Gauḍapāda

> That which is supported by *śruti* and corroborated by reason, that alone is the acceptable truth and none other.
>
> —*MK* III. 23

Gauḍapāda, while resorting to scripture throughout the text, makes use of reason and provides a rational approach to Advaita. Even his quotation of scripture often is a passage wherein arguments are given. He uses reasoning (*hetu*, *yukti* or *upapatti*) throughout the text in his efforts to show the illusoriness of the world of duality, to establish the non-illusoriness of non-dual Reality, and to show that the pluralistic views concerning creation are mutually contradictory and thus fallacious.

1. *MK* I. 29, II. 35; II. 1, 5; IV. 54; II. 31; II. 34; II. 35; IV. 19, 88; IV. 86; IV. 86; IV. 89; and IV. 95 respectively. From Mahadevan, *op. cit.*, p. 90. See also a list of phrases given by Bhattacharya, *op. cit.*, p. lxii.

As the above quotation indicates, Gauḍapāda gives reason a substantial place in his Advaita.[1] Reason is an aid in the selection and interpretation of scriptural passages wherein the Truth is disclosed.[2] Reason itself is unable to comprehend Ultimate Reality and it is also unable to lead the aspirant to its realization. It is only mediate knowledge but is able to assist enquiry and the pursuit of real knowledge.

On the level of philosophical enquiry, Gauḍapāda uses reason to show the intellectual absurdity of duality and the views which mirror this orientation and to firmly establish the truth of non-dual Reality. In the *Kārikā* there is a net-work of interwoven arguments for this purpose. The method on the whole is not a thoroughly systematic one, for Gauḍapāda passes from argument to argument and the connection is often tenuous, even in the face of Śaṅkara's masterly commentary.[3] The fourth *prakaraṇa* is by far the most cogent and systematic chapter. Herein Gauḍapāda uses the four-pronged dialectic (*catuṣkoṭi*) to the advantage of his final conclusion or position (*siddhānta*). Syllogistic forms are reconstructed by the commentators Śaṅkara and Ānandagiri.[4] The *anvayavyatireki* (inference based on the co-presence and co-absence of the probans and the probandum) mode of argumentation is used in several places.[5] Gauḍapāda also employs the method of argumentation known as *tarka* (*reductio ad absurdum*).[6] He uses analogical reasoning throughout the *Kārikā* and with great dexterity in showing the illusoriness of the waking world on the ground of its similarity with the world of the dream state.

---

1. Mahadevan, *op. cit.*, pp. 81-93.

2. "As a Vedāntist, he treats his subject in accordance with the scriptures (*śruti*), yet, not without pure reasons. Direct or indirect, his reasonings are in many cases based on scriptures (II. 1-10; III. 24-26). But when there are contradictory scriptures, he says (III. 23) that those which are with reasons (*yukti-yukta*) are to be accepted. Besides, throughout the work he has advanced a number of independent grounds which are very cogent." Bhattacharya, *op. cit.*, p. cxxvii.

3. Caterina Conio. *The Philosophy of the Māṇḍūkya Kārikā* (Varanasi : Bharatiya Vidya Bhavan, 1971), pp. 69-94 deals with the disjointed nature of Gauḍapāda's reasoning and argumentation in the work as a whole.

4. For example in the commentary on *MK* II. 14.

5. For example in *MK* II. 17-18 and III. 31.

6. *MK* I. 17-18.

Other comparisons are used, the most prominent of which are those concerned with illusion, such as the *fata morgana*, the magic-elephant, the rope-snake, and the designs created by the movement of the fire-brand, etc. Gauḍapāda also points out the fallacies in the arguments of other schools of thought.[1]

It is through these modes that Gauḍapāda has provided the philosophy of Advaita with a solid foundation upon which to build and develop.

When analyzing the *Māṇḍūkya Kārikā* from the perspective of Gauḍapāda as preceptor, other uses of reason can be seen. The aim of Advaita is not pure philosophy but pure experience. To a large extent it aims at the rejection of all philosophies, though not out of scepticism or antagonism, but by transcending them.

> The dualists, confirmed believers in the methodologies establishing their own conclusions, are at logger-heads with one another. But this (non-dual) view finds no conflict with them. Non-duality is the highest Reality, since duality is said to be a product of it. But for them there is duality either way. Therefore this view (of ours) does not clash (with theirs).[2]

The purpose of enquiry is basic in Advaita Vedânta. It consists in posing problems or doubts and seeking solutions for them. The problem in Advaita concerns the knowledge of *Brahman*, of Reality. Philosophically this becomes a matter of metaphysical understanding and religiously it is a matter of "knowing" and "becoming" that reality. These two are said to be one ultimately.

The "desire to know" is the first pre-requisite which Advaita Vedânta says is necessary for the aspirant (*sādhaka*). Traditionally he places himself under a preceptor (*guru*) and begins his

---

1. Some details are provided by Mahadevan, *op. cit.*, p. 91.

2. *MK* III. 17-18. "Advaita Vedânta is not interested in elaborating the ontological structures of being and in defining concepts and categories—rather to make a dialectical criticism thereof—based on the awareness that the concepts and categories being finite in character, cannot comprehend the infinite or the unconditioned being—they may be applicable in the realm of duality and the finite, but have no relevance so far as the awareness or experience of being is concerned." R.S. Misra, *Studies in Philosophy and Religion* (Varanasi : Bharatiya Vidya Prakasana, 1971), p. 6.

sādhanā or spiritual quest. The teacher instructs (*upadeśa*) the aspirant in the knowledge of Reality which provides him with the means to understand this intellectually to some degree so that he can eventually experience this directly for himself.

Here the preceptor uses scriptural authority (*śruti*) which enunciates the truths to corroborate his statements. For scripture is the highest source of mediate knowledge concerning spiritual matters. Then the teacher may show the falsity of phenomenal experience and point out the erroneous nature of the teachings of other schools through both scripture and reasoned argument. Along with this the practical advice for the full realization of *Brahma-vidyā* is given.

This is also called *vicāra*, the constant reflection and concentration on spiritual problems. This directly concerns the enquiry into the nature of Reality (*Brahman*) and the Self (*Ātman*). Reasoning by the student (*sādhaka*) aided by the explanations, arguments, examples and illustrations from the teacher, enables him to progress on the path towards Self-realization. This is the practical usage of philosophy within Advaita Vedānta.

In this way the philosophy in the sense of reasoned argumentation in its various forms becomes a practical teaching technique.[1] Reality is asserted and "illusion" is denied. These are demonstrated and defended through the use of scripture and reason. Through this method the aspirant learns basic teachings of the system and is able to understand and internalize them easily. Explanation of these various sorts are especially useful in that they are means to resolve the doubts and apprehensions of the aspirant concerning the possibility of the experience and that it is more adequate than that offered by other schools of thought.[2]

---

1. *MK* I. 18 : This kind of talk is for the sake of making instruction (*upadeśa*) possible.

2. "Does Gauḍapāda really try to give a logical foundation to the Upaniṣadic intuition, or does he merely try to illustrate it by example as any good *guru* does to help his pupil understand it? In other words, is Gauḍapāda's purpose a philosophical or a pedagogical one ? It is not obviously a question of determining the personal intentions of the compiler of the *kārikā*—though the religious motive is quite evident. It is a question of determining the philosophical character or otherwise, of the value of the given arguments." Conio, *op. cit.*, p. 3.

What the student has heard he must reflect upon (*manana*). He is to look at it critically from different perspectives and resolve any doubts which might assail him until he is convinced of the truth of what he has been taught. What he learns on the authority of scripture and his *guru* is to be meditated in thought before it can become a matter of personal intuitive experience. Through critical reflection lies the way to direct realization (*sākṣātkāra*).

Advaita Vedānta represents the *jñāna-mārga*, the path of knowledge, which holds that the immediate knowledge of one's *ātman* (Self) can be only through *aparokṣa-jñāna* (direct unmediated intuitive experience or knowledge). As has bean shown, the tradition makes use of the mediate forms of knowledge to aid in this realization.

> *Śruti* is what is helped; *yukti* or *tarka* is what helps. As an aid to revelation, reason is of inestimable value; and it should be regarded as subsidiary to *śruti* and *anubhūti*.[1]

4. Other Teaching Devices Used by Gauḍapāda

> Things to be rejected, realized, accepted, and made effective are to be known at the very beginning. —*MK* IV. 90

As is evident from this quotation, an entire practice is set forth for the *sādhaka* as well as its philosophical justification. Gauḍapāda provides both in the text of the *Māṇḍūkya Kārikā*. Although in written form, it still reflects the technique of personal conversation and dialogue of the oral upaniṣadic tradition. It merely takes a step out of the intimate *guru-śiṣya* (teacher-student) relationship and sets forth the process of instruction in a textual form. This difference of situation is reflected in the text in its overtures to systematic presentation and yet it retains the looseness of the intimate and secret verbal transmission in its structure, form, expressions, and methods.

Gauḍapāda, as has been shown, uses scripture, reason, and practical spiritual advice and at times these are specifically for use as *śravaṇa* (listening), *manana* (thinking) and *nididhyāsana*

---

1. Mahadevan, *op cit.*, p. 88, paraphrasing Śaṅkara's *Brahma Sūtra Bhāṣya* I.1.2 and II.1.6.

(contemplation). Within these forms he shows himself as adept at the use of figurative language. He utilizes poetic expression, mythological examples, sagacious analogies, examples and illustrations for the purposes of description and explanation. These are used philosophically to stimulate the intellect and also religiously to entice the heart of aspirant. For the highest truth or Ultimate Reality is beyond description, beyond language, beyond the intellect. It can only be indicated inadequately through language by pointing out some similarities to valued qualities, through analogous instances and negative pronouncements concerning its nature. In this way the language used exhibits a large degree of symbolic expression in these various forms.[1]

In the first *prakaraṇa* Gauḍapāda makes use of the mythological-symbolic figures representing the three states of experience to good advantage, for it concretizes what is a rather abstract concept of that total experience. His use of metaphors abounds throughout the whole text, the most notable of which are that of the fire-brand concerning the nature of the creation and the illusory nature of the manifested universe (IV. 47-50) and that of the space within the various jars concerning the nature of the individual souls (*jivas*) and *Brahman* (III.1-11 etc.).[2] In III.15, Gauḍapāda gives an instance of the use of the examples of earth, gold, sparks, and so forth in scripture to indicate the unity which exists within the multifarious creation. In many other instances, he merely follows the principles of explanation and instruction already used within the Upaniṣadic literature.

Gauḍapāda presents images, related to everyday experience, by which the aspirant may further understand the abstruse teachings. He explains things in ways understandable to the enquiring individual. For example, he talks of "creation"

1. An analogy's function lies in its suggesting a meaning which cannot be adequately formulated in thought. It is not to hint at a totally unexpressible reality but to symbolize something we do know, though not entirely. Thus it opens a door to deeper insight. This is especially seen in the taking of epistemological expressions into the metaphysical field.

2. Further, in *MK* III.14, Gauḍapāda says that the *karmakāṇḍa* portions of scripture use a figurative or secondary language (*gauṇa*) when they say that the *jīva* and *ātman* are different.

through the process of "imagination" : *Ātman*, to which he gives the concrete form of *Īśvara*, the Lord, "turns his mind outward" (III.13). He embellishes this with examples of dreaming, magic, illusion and hallucination. And in this way he enables the aspirant to perceive the process of creation and "turning back" (IV. 74) through this visual and familiar process of the mind.

These are all means of expressing and communicating religious or spiritual experience. It reveals the phenomenological versus the logical nature of Advaita. It is not so much a problem of defining *Brahman* etc. as it is one of describing the fundamental features of man's experience of Being. The experiential dimension is interpreted by the mind in to symbols, concrete descriptions and designations for the purposes of communication. The name, *Brahman*, for example, is the conceptual interpretation or objectification of the "content" of non-dualistic spiritual experience. Any description of this sort is limited by the structure of language and the content of everyday experience. As such it is merely a provisional and partial definition. But as *Brahman* is acosmic, the tradition prefers to describe it "*via negativa*", through terms like *acintyam* (beyond thought), *asparśam* (beyond contact), *aśabdam* (beyond speech), etc. What is implied therein is that the principle is indefinable in terms known to us. As it cannot be defined in terms of a "second", it is *advayam*, *advaitam*, *advitīyam* (non-dual). As it is incomparable, no finite word or thought can measure it, nor negate it.

For these reasons, Gauḍapāda's text is difficult to fully understand by the intellect alone.[1] In order to enable the student to understand here, as well as on other levels, Gauḍapāda talks from various perspectives to aid the student in coming to a comprehensive intellectual understanding and eventually to personal realization. Hence he writes paradoxically when making statements from the perspective of the highest knowledge (*paramārtha satya*). When writing from our everyday shared world of experience (*saṃvṛti*) he expresses these truths figuratively and experientially. Thus he switches back and forth between these two levels of understanding in his exposition. Also,

1. *MK* IV. 100.

it should be noted, that Gauḍapāda mostly expounds his teachings from the *pāramārthika* point of view, i.e., from the point of view of highest state of non-duality. This leads him into an enormous amount of negation and strong arguments concerning the nature of reality.

Finally, Gauḍapāda possesses an apt ability to comprehend the difference in intellectual capacities and capabilities of students and to prescribe for them an appropriate spiritual pursuit. This is called *upāya* or skilful means. Realizing that ordinary people find it difficult to grasp the subtle Truth of Advaita, Gauḍapāda recognizes the need for appropriate understanding and especially appropriate practice to suit the individual in his spiritual growth or evolution. Knowing that in the course of time they will be in a position to understand the highest Truth, Gauḍapāda allows the practice of different kinds of disciplines for those who are within the traditional stages of life (*āśramas*) (III.16) and for those therein who are graded as being of lower, middling and higher or superior abilities. Through time and assiduous practice anyone can progress in the spiritual life. He sanctions the use of any means to lead the individual to further growth and progress, be it in the form of lesser philosophical understanding or the practice of a lesser spiritual discipline. Through time, experience, right thinking, and proper advice the aspirant will evolve and eventually become Self-realized and thus find freedom, peace and bliss in this very life.

In sum, Gauḍapāda is seen to be a preceptor of great ability. Aware of the nature of Reality and the difficulty in communicating this in any forms he uses various modes and devices to enable others to come to some understanding of this intellectually and practically in direct, personal experience. Thus he harmoniously combines a mastery of scripture, logical skill, and rich spiritual experience in his *Māṇḍūkya Kārikā* exposition of the theory and practice of *Brahma-vidyā*.

Chapter IV

THE PHILOSOPHY OF GAUḌAPĀDA'S *MĀṆḌŪKYA KĀRIKĀ*

Hence I shall speak of that (*Brahman*) which is free from limitation, has no birth, and is in a state of equipoise; and listen how nothing whatsoever is born in any way, though it seems to be born.

—*MK* III. 2

In his dual role as a philosopher and preceptor, Gauḍapāda's function as a philosopher has been isolated to a large extent by scholars.[1] He is seen primarily as a metaphysician and the first systematic philosopher of the Advaita Vedānta tradition. This aspect of his life and work will be dealt with in this chapter while the remaining chapters will deal with the explicit though related aspects of Gauḍapāda's practical side as a preceptor. This chapter then will briefly sketch the main areas of his metaphysical concern. Beginning with his assumptions of the nature of non-dual Reality and the concept of *ajātivāda* (non-origination), the nature and relationship between non-duality and the world and the individual will be explored in turn.

1. Non-Duality (Advaita)

Brahman is birthless, sleepless, dreamless, nameless, formless, ever effulgent, everything, and a knower.

—*MK* III.36

1. This work has been done by scholars and the reader is directed to them, especially to T.M.P. Mahadevan's *Gauḍapāda : A Study in Early Adaita*, for further elucidation on the area of metaphysics and precise nature of the argumentation which is used therein.

Among the Vedāntins, Gauḍapāda is an Advaitin, the highest truth to him being *advaita* or "non-duality."[1] As with all Advaitins there are two main aspects of his teachings concerning reality. First, it is stated that the sole reality is the non-dual *Brahman*. Secondly, the pluralistic universe of common experience is illusory, false or deceptive. The definite conclusion of Vedānta is that only the non-dual *Brahman* exists and that everything is really *Brahman*. To perceive otherwise is due to ignorance of the nature of Reality.

Gauḍapāda assumes, or rather takes his philosophical and religious stand on, non-dual *Brahman* as the highest truth and supreme reality. This is both the teaching and the ultimate goal of his philosophy and advocated practice. The non-dual *Brahman* is not just a conceptual doctrine but rather the plenary experience which the individual aspirant must attain in order to be truly free and enlightened.

Gauḍapāda expounds this teaching concerning non-dual *Brahman* through quoting scriptural passages, through reasoning and through illustrations.

The *Āgama-prakaraṇa* itself embodies the relevant quotations of the *Māṇḍūkyopaniṣad*. Here the non-dual, unchanging Reality is called *Turiya*, "the fourth."[2] In the analysis of experience, the three *avasthās* are shown to subsist in this reality. It is not a fourth state of experience in addition to, or over and above the others, but is itself the one reality of which they are appearances. As it is not a finite entity it cannot really be described or even named. It is thus indirectly indicated by negative terms indicating what it is not. Thus it is said to be the cessation of the world, quiescent, blissful and non-dual. It is the Self which is *Brahman* and the scriptures refer to it by the sacred *mantra* *OM*.[3] In his attached *Kārikās*, Gauḍapāda expands on this doctrine of the *Turiya* while closely following the Upaniṣad.[4]

---

1. *Advaitam paramārthaḥ* (I.17); *advaitam paramārtho hi* (III. 18); *advaite yojayet smṛtim* (II. 36). There are indirect references throughout the text also.
2. *MUp* 7 and 12.
3. *MUp* 1, 2, 7, 8, and 12.
4. *MK* I. 10-16 especially.

The equivalence of *Turīya*, *Brahman*, *Ātman*, and the *praṇava* (*Oṅkāra*) is re-iterated.[1]

In the *Advaita-prakaraṇa* Gauḍapāda cites well-known passages from the Upaniṣads in order to indicate the scriptural basis of the teaching concerning non-dual *Brahman*.[2] The second and fourth *prakaraṇas* also add emphasis to this in their concern with showing the falsity and deception of plurality through reasoned argumentation.

The nature of *Brahman* is defined both affirmatively and negatively by Gauḍapāda, following the way of the Upaniṣads. Positively, *Brahman* is *Īśvara* or God when related to and inclusive of the world. In this form he is called the lower (*apara*) *Brahman* and is seated in the hearts of all.[3] He is the all-pervasive Lord, impelling all beings to activity.[4] *Īśvara* is equated with *Turīya* and the symbol *OM*. As such He is also the beginning, middle and end of all things[5] and remains the same within all the changing states of experience.[6] To him devotion and worship is given through the practice of *upāsanās* etc.

Negatively, *Brahman* cannot be designated nor described, for it is trans-phenomenal.[7] The higher *Brahman* (*parabrahma*)[8] is not related to this pluralistic universe in any way. Because of this the language used is a negation of dualistic designations. *Brahman* can really only be characterized as "not this, not this".[9] There is nothing prior to it; not anything after it. It has neither an inside nor an outside; no name, nor form; no content, nor movement.[10] It is devoid of sleep and dream and as the "fourth" transcends the three states of experience.[11]

---

1. *MK* I. 25-27.
2. The selections in the *Advaita-prakaraṇa* are drawn from the *Bṛh. Up.* in particular and especially book IV of that text. Also, *MK* IV. 12, 24, 25, 26 give specific reference through quotations.
3. *MK* I. 26 and 28.
4. *MK* I. 10.
5. *MK* I. 27.
6. *MK* I. 22.
7. *MK* IV. 60.
8. *MK* I. 26 and III. 12.
9. *MK* III. 26.
10. *MK* I. 26, III. 36, IV. 45 respectively.
11. *MK* I. 14, 16, III. 36, IV. 81.

In spite of the nature of these restrictions of description, Gauḍapāda does indicate some positive implications of this negation lest *Brahman* be inferred as a void or a non-entity. *Brahman* is eternal and infinite non-dual reality.[1] It is the self-luminous, all-light, pure consciousness which remains ever the same.[2] And it is said to be infinite bliss and tranquillity.[3] This description is in essence the definition of *Brahman* as *sat*, *cit*, and *ānanda* used later in the tradition.

2. Non-Origination (Ajātivāda)

> Since origination is not a well-established fact, it is declared (by the Upaniṣads) that everyting is birthless. Moreover, there is no origination, in any way whatsoever, of any non-existing thing from an existing one.
>
> —*MK* IV. 38

The central theme of Gauḍapāda's metaphysics is his doctrine of *ajātivāda*, that "nothing whatsoever is born".[4] This doctrine is intended by Gauḍapāda to show that non-duality is the supreme Truth. For from the standpoint of the Absolute (*Brahman*), there is no duality, nothing finite or non-eternal. *Brahman* alone is. All else is illusory and non-real appearance. Empirical distinctions are untrue, they are devoid of reality. Any idea of origination is mere illusion and non-origination is the ultimate truth.

Non-origination, non-birth , or the negation of the concept of causality strikes at the root of dualistic conceptual thought. The concept of birth or causation suggests duality in all its forms of relation. Cause and effect is the example which stands for the other relations within time, space and causality such as subject-object, substance-attribute, and so forth. Instead of dealing with multiple examples of dualistic relations, he confines himself to fully exploring this one proposition.

---

1. *MK* III. 18 and 33.
2. *MK* I. 12, III. 36, IV. 81.
3. *MK* I. 29, III. 47, IV. 93.
4. *MK* III. 48, IV. 38, and 71 are definite summation statements. It is also indicated in IV. 5, 19, 22, 29, 40, 45, 78, and 96.

Gauḍapāda expounds the philosophy of *ajāti* in the third and fourth *prakaraṇas* of the text. In the *Advaita-prakaraṇa*, Gauḍapāda draws support from scriptural passages. He admits that scripture (*śruti*) teaches creation (*sṛṣṭi*) in many places but he points out that scripture does not declare that it is real. Scripture also teaches the non-duality of the Self and the illusory nature of plurality. If creation were real, these latter teachings would themselves be fallacious. The real import and interpretation derived through proper inquiry (*niścita*) and reasoning (*yuktiyukta*) is that the creation which is spoken of must be an illusory one (*māyāmaya*).[1] The real purpose of the instances where scripture speaks of creation is to introduce the unity of the phenomenal manifistation which indicates its real nature as non-dual reality.[2] Gauḍapāda also admits that creation is spoken of for those who are afraid of this truth of non-birth and who as yet have not progressed on the spiritual path to the point of such an understanding.[3]

In the *Alātaśānti-prakaraṇa*, the last chapter of the work, Gauḍapāda gives a critique of causality and by means of dialectical arguments he attempts to show that the concept of origination is untenable. Again, that people ordinarily believe in the origination of things, Gauḍapāda does not deny. What he does do is to show that such a belief, when critically examined, lends itself to contradictions making it unintelligible. In *MK* IV.3, 4 and 5, he says that those who dispute with each other simply destroy each other's position and thus aid in establishing *ajātivāda* by their mutual contradiction.

At the end of the third *prakaraṇa*, Gauḍapāda also details the basic arguments for non-origination. He takes up the theories of causation held by the transformationists (*pariṇāmavādins*) in *MK* III.27 and the nihilists (*asadvādins*) in *MK* III.28. Those who subscribe to the view of transformation of original being into the world, that things take birth in a real sense, hold that there can only be the birth of what is already born. This, Gauḍapāda points out, is a contradiction. For when a thing is born

1. *MK* III. 23.
2. *MK* III. 15 and the following verses through to III. 28.
3. *MK* IV. 42 and 43.

it ceases to be birthless. What the disputants should say is that what is born is born as something else. This, however, is unsatisfactory as it leads the argument into becoming one of a never-ending process of seeking previous causes. The result of this is that one can only say that the birth of what already exists can be reasonably possible only through *māyā* and not in reality. The nihilist maintains that the world which appears is produced out of the unreal (*asat*), that the non-existent cannot be born either really (*tattvataḥ*), nor illusorily (*māyayā*). The example given is the classical one of the son of a barren woman. Thus, after examining these opposing views, Gauḍapāda states that the real alone may be said to be born, and even that is not in reality but only through *māyā*. In the second *prakaraṇa* Gauḍapāda previously explained this on the analogy of the dream-world. As in the dream state, a world is created illusorily, so also in waking a similar thing happens. In *MK* III.29 and 30 he goes further and suggests that it is the mind which moves through *māyā* and creates the illusion of the dual distinctions of the pluralistic universe. The distinctions of seer, seen, cause and effect, etc. create the appearance of a real world. The ultimate truth is that there is nothing which is born and that Reality is unborn (*aja*) and non-dual (*advaya*).[1]

The main dialectical argument that all is *aja* and that the origination of anything cannot be demonstrated is given several times.[2] In *MK* IV. 22, IV. 38 and 40, the argument that in no way can the generation of anything be demonstrated follows thus :

1. the non-existent cannot have the non-existent for its cause,
2. nor the existent have the non-existent for its cause,
3. the existent cannot be the effect of the existent,
4. nor can the existent be the effect of the non-existent.

---

1. Corroborated by Śaṅkara's and Ānandagiri's commentaries on *MK* III. 27.

2. *MK* IV. 22, 38, and 83-4. This dialectic is used by Gauḍapāda throughout the fourth *prakaraṇa*. For example, it can be seen within the arguments used in *MK* III. 20-22 and IV. 6-10, IV. 11-19, IV. 24-28 and so on.

The cause-effect relation is thus seen to be replete with contradictions when put to careful analysis.

Gauḍapāda also uses illustrations in the last *prakaraṇa* not only to show that reality is non-dual (*advaita*) but that non-origination (*ajāti*) is the highest truth. He uses the analogy of dreams in IV. 32-41 to show that the waking state is non-real and thus un-originated. Verses 47-50 give the important illustration of the fire-brand wherein the designs are not in fact truly formed by the moving fire-brand and that like the things of the phenomenal universe they are not really created. Other examples suggest that as the snake is not at any time born of the rope, and the sky-city is not created by an architect, nor the magic-elephant really generated, the apparent birth and death of things are likewise illusory.[1] The highest truth, states Gauḍapāda, is that nothing whatsoever is born.[2]

Here, as with *Turīya* and *Brahman*, even to give a designation to this non-dual principle is in fact to distort the truth of it itself. For *ajāti* is meaningful only as long as *jāti* (birth) carries a meaning within everyday empirical dealings.[3] Just as *Turīya* is called the "fourth" through the super-imposition of a number category for the purpose of indicating the subtle difference from the three *avasthās*, so also is *ajāti* spoken of erroneously to this degree in order to enable the student to understand the subtle distinction of this reality from what appears to be born.

Brahman is not born, nor is there anything else that is born. *Brahman*, which is the eternal and immutable Reality, is neither effect nor cause. There is nothing other than it, either to produce it or be produced by it. Origination (*jāti*), activity (*calatva*), and objectivity (*vastutva*) are all false appearances.[4]

There is no dissolution, no origination, none in bondage, none striving or aspiring for salvation, no seeker after release, and no one who is liberated. This, says Gauḍapāda, is the highest truth of Advaita Vedānta.[5] These expressions have meaning only in the relative world of experience (*saṃvṛti*) and make no sense

1. MK IV. 44, 68-70 and 71.
2. *MK* III. 48 and IV. 71.
3. *MK* IV. 74.
4. *MK* IV. 45.
5. *MK* II. 32.

sub specie aternitatis, for they have no place in the Absolute (*paramārtha*).

3. The Nature of the World

> All this duality that is nothing but *Māyā*, is but non-duality in reality. —*MK* I.17

Gauḍapāda speaks from the level of *paramārtha-satya* (absolute truth) when he states that the non-dual *Brahman* is the sole reality and the world of plurality is an illusory appearance induced by *māyā* (nescience or ignorance). From this perspective, he asserts that there is in reality no world and hence there is really no question as to the mode of its generation. The real (*sat*) is *prapañcopaśama*, the quiescence of the manifold universe.[1] If the universe appears it is an illusory manifestation. This view of the false or non-real nature of the world (*vaitathya*) came to be called *vivarta-vāda* in later Advaita.

Gauḍapāda uses several terms to express this illusory nature of the phenomenal world. *Māyā* is that which covers reality and projects the non-real world.[2] *Vaitathya*, as the name of the second *prakaraṇa* indicates, is unreality or that which is not the real (*sat*, i.e., *Brahman*).[3] *Mithyā* suggests that the world is fallacious due to being erroneously cognized. It is also referred to as an appearance (*ābhāsa*), that which is wrongly imagined (*kalpita*),[4] and an erroneous perception (*viparyaya*).[5] Contrasted with *Brahman*, the Absolute Reality (*paramārtha*), the reality which belongs to the world is empirical or relative (*vyāvahārika* or *saṃvṛti*).[6]

Gauḍapāda states his position in the first two *prakaraṇas*. In the *Āgama-prakaraṇa*, he establishes through *tarka* (*reductio ad absurdum*) that the universe does not really exist.[7] In the *Vaitathya-prakaraṇa*, he characterizes the world of waking to be illusory on the basis

1. *MUp* 7 and 12; *MK* I. 29 (*advaitasyopaśamaḥ*) and II. 35 (*prapañcopaśamaḥ*).
2. *MK* I. 17-18.
3. Śaṅkara's commentary on *MK* II. 1.
4. *MK* I. 18; II. 9, 10, 14 and 15.
5. *MK* IV. 46.
6. *MK* IV. 57 and 74.
7. *MK* I. 17-18.

of its similarities to the dream-world.[1] Gauḍapāda also utilizes many analogies and illustrations to further explain the illusoriness of the phenomenal world. For example, the well-known rope-snake analogy is given as well as the many illustrations of things created by magic (*māyā*). Though they appear, they do not truly exist. They are *māyā-mātra*, the production of magic-like *māyā* and thus mere illusion.

What then is the agency by which the manifold appearance is generated ? Gauḍapāda provides four answers from differing perspectives :

1. the Self (*Ātman*) imagines (*kalpana*) itself through itself[2]
2. the birthless Self becomes differentiated through *māyā*[3]
3. the world manifestation is a mere vibration of consciousness (*cittaspandita*)[4] as is perceived by the mind (*manodṛśya*)[5]
4. the Lord (*prabhu*) diversifies the mundane things turning His mind outward.[6]

Thus Gauḍapāda states that the Self, *Māyā*, Mind and God are responsible for the manifestation of the manifold universe.

In *MK* II. 12,13 and 19, Gauḍapāda brings these various perspectives together. As the Self is unchanging and eternal, it cannot of itself manifest anything or be the cause of anything. It is only the substratum or ground of the apparent manifestation of the world through *māyā*.[7] The Self conditioned by *māyā* is the cause of the plural universe. *Brahman* or the Self thus conditioned is called *Īśvara*, the Lord. Only God has relations with the world and is thus the efficient and material cause of the universe. It is the Lord, who creates or imagines the external things and the inter-

1. *MK* II. 1-11.
2. *MK* II. 12.
3. *MK* III. 19.
4. *MK* IV. 72.
5. *MK* III. 31.
6. *MK* II. 13. In II. 16 Gauḍapāda gives a few details concerning creation. First the *jīva* is posited then all the objects, external and internal. See also *MK* I.6.
7. See also *MK* III. 24 and 27.

nal modes by turning His mind outward.[1] By whatever agency and in whichever manner, the creation of the universe is not real from the *paramārtha* perspective, being only an illusory manifestation due to *māyā*. The objects that constitute the universe are non-real, only they appear as real.[2] In truth they cannot be declared as either real or non-real.

Māyā is thus the creative and illusive principle. It does not have an independent ontological status as it is not an entity or a reality having a substance of its own. *Brahman* is the only real (*sat*). As such, *māyā* is a riddle to the intellect. It is indeterminable and unthinkable.[3] But when the Absolute is directly realized in *anubhava*, there is no *māyā* to be explained, for *māyā* does not really exist.[4]

4. The Individual

> The fact that the non-difference of the individual and the supreme Self is extolled by a statement of their identity, and the fact that diversity is condemned, become easy of comprehension from this point of view alone.
>
> —*MK* III. 13

The *Māṇḍūkyopaniṣad* states in the second verse that "All this is surely *Brahman*. This Self is that *Brahman*." *Brahman* and *Ātman* are non-different from each other.[5] The true Self of each individual is the Absolute. The apparent finitude and individuality of the *jiva* (self) is due to *māyā*. Gauḍapāda shows this using the analogies of the space (*ākāśa*) within the jars,[6] the *kośas* or coverings,[7] and creatures formed of dream, or by magic, or through super-normal powers.[8] He says, "Birth, death, individuality, etc. are all illusory."[9] Through ignorance alone does

1. More details concerning the "mind" and its role in the creation of the manifold universe will be given in Chapter 5.
2. *MK* II.6, 30-31 and 34.
3. *MK* IV. 41 and 52.
4. *MK*. IV. 57 and 58.
5. *MK* III.13 and 14.
6. *MK* III.3-10.
7. *MK*. III.11 with reference to the elaboration in *Taitt. Up*. II. 1-4.
8. *MK* IV. 68-71.
9. *MK* III. 48.

the Self wrongly identify itself with the changing phenomena of the not-Self and thus is mistaken to be many and finite. Gauḍapāda accepts the empirical plurality of *jīvas* but adamantly maintains the oneness of the Self (*ekātma-vāda*).[1] For the higher Self (*ātman*) there is neither birth nor death, neither action nor enjoyment. These conditions only refer to the finite individual *jīvas* which are multiple.[2]

The distinctions are analogous to those which are seen in the space within the jars. Form, purpose and name may vary according to the limiting conditions. The psycho-physical conditions related to the individual *jīva* make no difference to its nature as the ever-liberated Self (*ātman*). They are absolutely non-different, being neither a mode nor portion, nor a transformation, nor modification of *Ātman*. The Self, then, is declared to be the non-dual, eternal and immutable Absolute Reality (*ayam ātmā brahma*).[3]

5. Liberation

> No soul ever came under veil. They are by nature pure as well as illumined and free from the very beginning. Thus being endowed with the power (of knowledge), they are said to know.
>
> —*MK* IV. 98

Mokṣa or liberation is the supreme goal of man according to Advaita. Gauḍapāda defines it as the realization of the truth of the Self (*ātmasatyānubodha*).[4] The individual realizes the non-difference of the *jīva* from the *Ātman* and attains the fullness of non-dual Being.[5] Ignorance (*avidyā* or *māyā*) vanishes completely. Self-realization is true perfection, freedom, release, bliss and peace. It is the final and complete end of life realizable while in embodiment rather than after death.[6]

Mokṣa is the eternal and inalienable nature of man. It is not something which has to be accomplished or attained some time

1. *MK* IV. 91 and 98.
2. *MK* III. 3-9 and IV. 68-71.
3. *MUp* 2.
4. *MK* III. 32.
5. *MK* III. 13 and II. 36.
6. *MK* IV. 89.

in the future. It is already there and has always been there. What is called liberation can only be attained figuratively. For release is really the re-discovery of what is already there. The path to this attainment or re-discovery is *jñāna* (direct knowledge or experience). It is through the "unborn knowledge" that the "unborn Self" is realized.[1]

It is for the aim and purpose of *mokṣa* for which the system devises its philosophy and practice. For *mokṣa* is not an intellectual concept but the ideal of life. The true Self is the experiential core of man. But, that man cannot "know" and "be" that center, he suffers in the world (*duḥkha*). Advaita Vedānta purports to outline this situation and, of more importance, provides the practical advice and techniques by which this state of Being may be fully discovered or realized by the aspiring individual.

1. *MK* IV. 96.

CHAPTER V

THE PHENOMENOLOGY AND META-PSYCHOLOGY OF THE *MĀṆḌŪKYA KĀRIKĀ*

> Those objecs that appear as obscure inside the mind, and those that appear as vivid outside, are all merely created by imagination. Their distinction is to be traced to the difference in the organs of perception.
>
> —*MK* II.15

> As in dream the mind vibrates, as though having dual aspects, so in waking state the mind vibrates as though with facets.
>
> —*MK* III.29

> All this that there is—together with all that moves or does not move—is perceived by the mind, (and therefore all this is but the mind); for when the mind ceases to be mind, duality is no longer perceived.
>
> —*MK* III.31

This chapter will outline an area of Gauḍapāda's thought which has been somewhat neglected and yet is vitally important for an analysis and understanding of his soteriological concern. This area is what could be called his "Meta-psychology," for Gauḍapāda's ontology, epistemology, soteriology, and his psychology meet here.

Four areas will be explored. First, Gauḍapāda's analysis of experience will be briefly explained. Then, his assumptions concerning the psychological structure and processes within man and the nature of consciousness will be examined. Next, the theories concerning "mind creation" will be looked at. And finally, the soteriological aspects of this meta-psychology will be indicated.

1. The Analysis of Experience

> I bow to that *Brahman* which after having enjoyed (during the waking state) the gross objects by pervading all the human objectives through a diffusion of Its rays of unchanging Consciousness that embraces all that moves or does not move; which again after having drunk (during the dream state) all the variety of objects, produced by desire (as well as action and ignorance) and lighted up by the intellect, sleeps while enjoying bliss and making us enjoy through *Māyā*; and which is counted as the Fourth from the point of view of *Māyā*, and is supreme, immortal, and birthless.
>
> —Śaṅkara's opening invocation to the *Kārikā*

Advaita Vedānta purports to be an experientially based religio-philosophical system. The meeting-point of the content of philosophy, religion and psychology is within man's consciousness. The body-mind complex of man is the laboratory for analysis and discovery in this school, whose main concern is to analyse and understand the complete nature of man.

Gauḍapāda's *Māṇḍūkya Kārikā* reflects this central concern in Advaita Vedānta since both theory and practice are based on experience. Gauḍapāda's philosophy analyzes and explains the inquiry into the nature of experience. His religious or spiritual prescriptions are also based on the results of the practical metaphysical pursuit.

The rational method of the analysis of all the states of man's experience is for the first time systematically pursued in Vedānta by Gauḍapāda in his *Kārikā*. This consists of an analysis of the three states of waking, dream, and deep sleep and the co-ordination of the experiences of these states. The method purports to be a comprehensive view of the dimensions of human experience as it attempts to analyse all possible states rather than being based on the waking state alone. It is an evaluation of the basic features of each state and a re-estimation of what is fundamental to each. Also, on the basis of this evaluation, there is to be a new assimilation of knowledge and experience, for the highest truth must be known directly. The analysis thus provides both a theoretical understanding and a method for experiencing the spiritual center of man.

Gauḍapāda bases his analysis of experience directly on the *Māṇḍūkyopaniṣad.* In doing so, he also makes the fullest use of the similar analyses found in the *Bṛhadāraṇyaka* and the *Chāndogya* Upaniṣads.[1] These examinations are summarized, synthesized and developed further by Gauḍapāda.

The *Māṇḍūkyopaniṣad* itself is concerned with the inquiry into the true nature of the Self (*ātman*). The analysis of the states of experience is employed with the aim of showing the non-duality of the Self which is found to be *Brahman* or *Turīya.* The basic question asked by the Upaniṣad is : is there in fact any fundamental, single Truth behind the evanescent plurality cognized by experience around us ? Thus it is concerned with disentangling the substratum or ground of experience from its complex manifestation. Its main contention is that the *Ātman*, the Self, which is the source of "I", the experiencer, is that principle which is the common denominator of the three states and that it remains unchanged and identical within them all.

Gauḍapāda follows the structure and the conclusions of this analysis in his commentary-like exposition within the first *prakaraṇa* of the *Māṇḍūkya Kārikā.* The remaining chapters of the text are based on the analysis and the findings of this examination. The second chapter, for example, attempts to show the illusory nature of the world of plurality. It begins with the thesis that the waking state is as unreal and delusory as the dream-world of seeming experience.[2] The third chapter details the advice on meditation based on the analysis, understanding and conclusions of this examination. The fourth *prakaraṇa* re-iterates the theory of the three states and *Turīya* but uses different terminology.[3]

Essentially, then, Gauḍapāda takes the total realm of human experience as his "unit of life" to be studied. He posits the factors of experience, the states of experience, and analyzes each according to the nature of the experiencer, the field of activity and

1. In *Bṛh. Up.* IV. 3.3 and in *Ch. Up.* V. 12-18, VIII. 6. 3, and II. 1 in particular.

2. *MK* II. 1-10.

3. *MK* IV. 87-89. The expressions appear to be those used in Buddhist literature.

the things enjoyed therein. The factors of experience, he says, are the experiencer, the experienced, and the experiencing itself.[1] Empirical experience is based on the relationship between the subject and its object. For all empirical dealings this triad of knowledge is fundamental. All phenomenal experience is thus of a dualistic structure, be it of an object experienced by a subject, or the opposition of two terms set apart and related each to the other.

The states (*avasthās*) of experience are three in number.[2] They are the state of "waking" (*jāgrat* or *laukika*),[3] the "dream" state (*svapna* or *śuddha-laukika*),[4] and the state of "deep sleep" (*suṣupti* or *lokottara*).[5]

The state of "waking" (*jāgrat*) is the everyday, shared world of phenomenal experience. Gauḍapāda uses the mytho-symbolic description of *Vaiśvānara* or *Viśva* to explain this state.[6] *Viśva* is said to be the ego-state here. He is really the Self (*Ātman*) identifying with this "outward" mode of consciousness (*bahiḥprajñaḥ*).[7] As "awareness directed to things outside", he is said to be possessed of nineteen "mouths" which are the five senses of perception, the five organs of action, the five vital forces, plus *manas* (the mind), *buddhi* (the intellect), *ahaṅkāra* (the ego), and *citta* (the mind-stuff). Thus *Viśva* is the enjoyer of the diverse gross objects of the phenomenal universe.[8]

Svapna, the "dream-state" is called *Taijasa* here. He is the experiencer or ego-state which is "aware of the internal objects"

---

1. *MK* II.29, 30; IV. 61, 62, 87 and 88.
2. *MUp* 1-5; *MK* I.9 and following verses; *MK* IV. 87-89.
3. *MUp* 3; *MK* II. 14 and IV. 87.
4. *MUp*. 4; *MK* II. 1, 3, 4 etc. and IV. 87.
5. *MUp* 5; *MK* III. 34, 35, and IV. 88.
6. Gauḍapāda concretizes the rather abstract conception of the total experience of each state by giving it a mytho-symbolic personality. Thus the reference to each state with a personal pronoun.
7. *MUp* 3; *MK* I. 1.
8. "In the state of waking, the self is conscious of what is without. The external world is its field of knowledge and enjoyment. The out-turned sense-organs are the channels of experience. The ego is set over against the non-ego. The former enjoys the latter; and the enjoyment is gross in nature because it is of the objects of the outer world. The individual soul, which thus resides in the physical body and uses the mind and the organs of sense as its instruments, is identical with the world soul." Mahadevan, *op. cit.*, p.97.

(*antaḥprajñaḥ*).[1] For in dream the senses are at rest and only the mind (*manas*) is active. Through the impressions left on the senses by the waking state it knows "objects". These objects are then "internal" or "subtle" in that they exist only subjectively in the form of mental modes. Although there is no other entity present here than the mind of the dreamer, the experiences appear as real as those of the waking state. Also, while in this state of experience, the factors of subject and object and the characteristics of externality and internality appear to be present.

The experiences of the waking and dream states are thus of the same nature, for in both the characteristics of perception are the same. From the standpoint of dream, dream objects are as gross and material as those experienced in the waking state. But, from the view-point of the waking state alone, it is inferred that the dream objects are in fact not gross objects at all, but rather only subjective modes of experience.

The third state of "deep sleep" (*suṣupti*) is called *Prājña*. *Prājña* is "a mass of consciousness" in that he is the experiencer or consciousness which remains in deep sleep. Though there are no specific states of objective consciousness here, there still is this "consciousness" per se which is said to be a unified self-luminous mass. He alone has the peculiar characteristics of undiversified consciousness, or of consciousness without objects. He is the subject without an object and yet he is also said to be the "doorway" to the other states of consciousness. The state represented here is not really the "dissolution" of the subject-object complex, but only a "dissociation", as duality has only ceased until the state of dream or that of waking again manifests.[2]

These are the three basic realms of human experience. Any other examples can be subsumed under one of these categories by a comparison of characteristics. This can be easily done, as the examination is also a phenomenology of consciousness which sug-

1. *MUp*. 4. Note that he is internal in relation to the senses.

2. The manifold implications of the conclusions of this analysis will not be dealt with here for lack of space. Suffice it to say that the metaphysics and transcendental experience of Advaita Vedānta are based or justified mainly on these epistemological or phenomenological grounds.

gests a categorization of the basic kinds or types of "consciousness". Following the above analysis they are :

1. the outward or objective (empirical) consciousness which appears only in the waking state,
2. the inward or subjective sphere of consciousness of dream and the like states of consciousness,
3. the un-consciousness (versus non-consciousness) of the deep sleep-like states.

This categorization further adds what can be called "pure consciousness." This is "the fourth," *Turiya*, the Consciousness underlying and yet transcending the three states of consciousness. It is the ever-present "witness" of all experience which is never annulled in any state. It is said to be the one Consciousness of which the others are metaphorically called "modes" due to the basic ignorance of the real nature of the subject of all experience. The three states have for their perceiver or experiencer, not three different personalities or ego-centers, but only one experiencer having three different names due to the inherent differences of each state of experience.[1]

Śaṅkara summarizes this in his commentary :

> In the three states, namely, waking etc., the one and the same object of experience appears in threefold forms as the gross, the subtle and the blissful. Further, the experiencer (of the three states) known (differently) as *Viśva*, *Taijasa*, and *Prājña* has been described as one on account of the unity of consciousness implied in such cognition as, " I am that" (common to all conditions), as well as from the absence of any distinction in respect of the perceiver. He who knows the two (experiencer and the objects of experience), appearing as many in the form

1. *MK* I. 1 and 2. "Thus, when I can remember all three planes of consciousness through which I traversed during the 24 hours of life, certainly there must be one common experiencer who was living through the three planes of experiences in me. The denominator or factor, who is the common experiencer in three fields of my activity, is the common I, the Eternal Factor, the Pure Consciousness." Swāmi Chinmayānanda, *Discourses on the Māṇḍūkya Upanishad with Gauḍapāda's Kārikā* (Madras : Chinmaya Publication Trust. 1953), p. 51.

of subject and objects of experience, though enjoying them, is not affected thereby; because all objects (of experience) are experienced by one subject alone. As (the heat of the fire) does not increase or decrease by consuming wood etc., so also nothing is added to or taken away (from the knowingness or awareness of the *Ātman*) by its experience of that which is its object.[1]

This "pure consciousness," the substratum and "witness" or experiencer of the three states is identified as *Turīya* in both the *Māṇḍūkyopāniṣad* and the *Māṇḍūkya Kārikā*.[2] *Turīya* is said to be non-different or the same as the designations *Brahman* and *Ātman*. Thus it represents the highest Truth, the supreme Reality, only it is the so-called "fourth" from the perspective of this analysis of the states of experience.

They consider the Fourth to be that which is not conscious of the internal world, nor conscious of the external world, nor conscious of both the worlds, nor a mass of consciousness, nor simple consciousness, nor unconsciousness; which is unseen, beyond empirical dealings, beyond the grasp (of the organs of action), uninferable, unthinkable, indescribable; whose valid proof consists in the single belief in the Self; in which all phenomena cease; and which is unchanging, auspicious, and non-dual. That is the Self, and that is to be known.[3]

This is a description of *Turīya* indicated by the language of negation or contrast to the other three states of consciousness. The second half of the verse also enumerates several positive qualities through this negation. *Turīya* is described as essentially a negation of sense-perception, the world of thought and ideas cognized through the instruments of the mind and intellect, and other limited forms of consciousness. It is the negation, as it were, of the objects (internal and external) of experience as well as their fields of experience. Thus, the text indicates that "the

1. Śaṅkara's commentary on *MK* I.5 (Swāmī Nikhilānanda's translation, *op. cit.*, p. 36.).
2. *MUp* 2, 7, 8, and 12; *MK* I. 10-16 especially.
3. *MUp* 7.

fourth" or the Self is not an "object", nor an "entity", nor an idea or concept, nor even a "state", but rather the ever-present "subject," "observer," "witness," or "substratum" which allows for "sentience," "intelligence," "vitality," and "experience."[1]

Turiya is thus the Self, the non-dual *Brahman* which on account of *Māyā* appears as the experient in the various states of experience. Although the experiences of the three states radically differ from one another, there is the knowledge that it is the same "I" or experiencer which was asleep and dreamt and is now awake. These states alternate, change and pass away while the *Turiya* remains ever constant through the varying states of mind. It is the changeless in the midst of change, the still point in the turning world. It is not caught in the triple stream of experience, though it is their underlying substrate or locus. *Turiya* ever remains unaffected and unattached by this world play (*prapañca*). Thus it is described as *advaita* (non-dual), *śānta* (quiescent), *śiva* (auspicious) and *prapañcopaśama* (the cessation of the pluralistic universe). This is the Consciousness which makes all experience possible.

The philosophy of Advaita assumes this central point of all existence and evaluates the spheres of experience from that absolute standard or standpoint. This gives rise to the analysis of experience into *paramārtha* and *vyavahāra* or *saṃvṛti*. These are the fundamental levels or modes of being. *Paramārtha* is that which is real (*sat*), ie., that which cannot be sublated, denied, or contradicted by any other experience. It refers to that *Turiya*, the witnessing Self, which is disclosed in the highest form or quality of human experience.[2]

1. "Either we know *of* a sound or such other sense perceptions, or *of* feelings or *of* our thoughts, but we do not know the *knowledge* by which we perceive, by which we understand our feelings, by which we know our ideas. . . Reality is Knowledge *as such*, wherein it has no objects to qualify. It is Pure Awareness in the light of which all other sense-organs go about their routine work of illuminating their individual objects." Swāmi Chinmayānanda, *op.*. cit., p.74.

2. "By the criterion of sublation, then, Reality is that which is when the subject-object situation is transcended. The Real is that which is the content of non-dual spiritual experience. It is the timeless-unconditioned, undifferentiated oneness of being. The Real is (*nirguṇa*) *Brahman.*" Eliot Deutsch, *Advaita Vedānta : A Philosophical Reconstruction* (Honolulu : East-West Centre Press, 1969), p. 19.

"That which is real or not-real" is now seen from another perspective or viewpoint. Anything which is other than this becomes mere "appearance." If something can be sublated in any way at all it is accordingly "disvalued". In this way, the manifold or pluralistic phenomenal universe is declared to be *saṃvṛti* or relative. The content of "sense-mental experience" within the subject-object situation is attributed a lesser degree of reality. Although every datum of experience within this appearance is "existent" rather than "unreal," it is still called "non-real" in that as sublatable it lacks full reality. Thus is the nature of the world determined by experience and also valued by the criterion of sublation.

In conclusion, Gauḍapāda bases his philosophy and practice on experience. Rather than piling explanations, he invites the aspirant to reflect upon what is experientially available to all. This knowledge is not theoretical but based on personal observation. The aim of Advaita here is to point out the wider meaning of experience as going beyond the relative into a trans-empirical experience not of "man" but of the "witnessing Self" or "Experiencer." This synthesis of psychological and philosophical investigation is the foundation of Advaita metaphysics and spiritual practice.

2. Gauḍapāda's Psychology : The Nature of the Mind

> *Viśva* experiences the external things and is all-pervading; but *Taijasa* experiences the internal things; similarly, *Prājña* is a mass of consciousness. It is but the same entity that is thought of in three ways.
>
> —*MK* I.1

Gauḍapāda's analysis of the states of experience (*avasthās*) also reveals a working psychology of Advaita Vedānta. Consciousness is the ground of experience. This consciousness as the witnessing Self is present throughout all phases of experience. It is said to be man's true spiritual nature. Thus man is seen to be a psycho-physical being whose true nature is spiritual.

Man is literally spirit within matter. In the analysis of the five sheaths (*kośas*) which Gauḍapāda alludes to in *MK* III. 11, he indicates this understanding of man. The *kośas* are like so many covering vestures which the Self (*Ātman*) wears while revealing itself in the world. This philosophical anatomy gives five sheaths or coverings which are :

1. *annamaya*, the physical body which is the locus of action and enjoyment;
2. *prāṇamaya*, the vital sheath which is manifest in the form of breath, the principle of animation and energy;
3. *manomaya*, the mind which consists of desires;
4. *vijñānamaya*, having the power of cognition it is of the nature of the agent and is responsible for all empirical knowledge both in waking and dream states;
5. *ānandamaya*, the mode of bliss.

These are respectively the gross and subtle encasings which cover the Self within each individual.

Spirit and matter are thus the two extremes of man's being. Gauḍapāda accepts the *Māṇḍūkyopaniṣad* account of man's psycho-physical complex.[1] Man consists of :

1. the five organs of perception (*buddhīndriyas*), i.e., the organs of sight, sound, smell, taste and touch;
2. the five organs of action (*karmendriyas*), i.e., the hands, feet, the organs of speech, generation, and evacuation;
3. the five aspects of the vital breath (*prāṇa*) ;
4. the mind (*manas*) ;
5. the intellect (*buddhi*) ;
6. egoity (*ahaṅkāra*) ;
7. the mind-stuff (*citta*).

These are the "mouths" or instruments by means of which the Self experiences the outward and inward dimensions of experience. The experiencer is seen to be of the greatest importance in this complex. It is the most subtle and that aspect of this psycho-physical complex which remains when each factor is withdrawn. For it is seen that man exists subjectively in the dream-like states when the out-going senses are at rest. Even this subsides when the individual is in deep sleep. The Vedāntins, seeing that

1. *MUp* 2-7; *MK* I. 1-6 and II. 16.

the Self remains after the other factors of man's makeup are withdrawn, have accorded it the highest place. For it is the Self which remains, the basis of all experience, and that which is not amenable to sublation. Moreover, it is this Self which illumines the other factors with its sentience.

The center of experience in the three states is the psychic or mental complex of man, i.e., the "mind" as a whole. The *manas*, *buddhi*, *ahaṅkāra*, and *citta* are but designations of the various functions of this "internal organ" which later Vedānta called the *antaḥkaraṇa*. Often, as here in the *Māṇḍūkya Kārikā*, this is simply designated as *manas*, the "mind."

Narrowly defined, the *manas* is an organ which is of subtle matter and of limited size. It ranks as an internal sense-organ and is that which governs the other outer sense-organs. The ten *indriyas* work under the control of *manas*, the central or internal sense-organ. These are dependent on *manas* for their functioning and through the coordination of *manas* the individual has perceptual knowledge. Because of this, the *manas* taken in this specific sense, is said to be only an instrument of knowledge for the experiencing Self (*Ātman*).

Besides this restricted definition, *manas* again represents the "internal organ of knowledge" as a whole. It is the integrating instrument of knowledge for the Self. As the *ahaṅkāra* function of this internal organ, *manas* becomes the individual "self" or "ego," known as the *jiva*. The *jīva* is responsible for, or literally "possesses", the empirical knowledge which arises when the mind and the external sense-organs function. This is so through the relation of "mind" and "consciousness."[1] Through the process designated later in the tradition as "super-imposition" (*adhyāsa*), and here called *māyā*, *vikalpa*, etc. by Gauḍapāda, the "mind" or "empirical self" as subtle insentient matter (i.e., as object) is attributed with sentience or consciousness (as the subject). In this way, "Consciousness" and the "mind" or "self" are one and the same.

The danger here is that of a complete and erroneous identification of consciousness with the empirical mind. This is the

1. *MK* IV. 45-52, 54, 61-66, 72, 77, 79-81.

crux of the bondage-release problem for Advaita Vedānta. Pure Consciousness is a contentless consciousness in which there is no consciousness of either "I" (*aham*) or "this" (*idam*) whereas the mind has no connotation without this subject-object relationship. The *ahaṅkāra* or empirical self is said to assume the center point of experience erroneously and through this false identification becomes thoroughly enmeshed in objective and subjective experience wherein it is bound and suffers.[1]

From the point of view that everything is consciousness, *manas* and the other empirical things cannot be different from it. But from the perspective of the objective experience of these, they cannot be really identified with consciousness per se. It is only for the practical purposes of life that Advaita uses "consciousness" to denote the knowledge relation of the Self with its objects. It is in this context that it is said, when the Self or pure Consciousness becomes limited by adjuncts, it is known as the individual *ātman*, the *jiva*, which is the knower and to whom knowledge is supplied by means of the organs of knowledge and sensations. Yet, it is strongly maintained that the distinction of knower, known, and the process of knowledge does not exist for the higher Self.[2] The Self is of the nature of pure non-dual Consciousness, the substratum of all experience, all manifestation. In this way *manas* can be viewed from the two levels of truth. Gauḍapāda uses this word play to good advantage particularly when talking of the nature of the Self and the method by which to attain it.

The nature of perceptual knowledge within this context is important here. For on the one hand, *jñāna* or knowledge is said to be non-dual and, on the other hand, perceptual knowledge functions within the dualistic sphere of subject-object relationships. It is *manas* which determines the nature of knowledge. Perception is immediate knowledge which is possible

1. In his commentary on *MK* II. 17 Śaṅkara remarks that the imagination or appearance of the individual *jiva* is the root of all other imaginations (*jīva-kalpanā sarvakalpanā-mūlam*). This is a further reference to *MK* II. 16 which suggests that the empirical self is first and then are imagined the various entities, both objective and subjective.

2. *MK* IV. 88-90.

only of objects which are directly present and which are tangible enough to be perceived. Mind as the subject and the objects of perception are interdependent and determine one another.[1] Every knowledge situation involves the threefold division of the knower, the process of knowing and the object known. Perceptual knowledge is manifested to the mind by getting into contact with the external object through sense-perception or in its mode as a *citta-vṛtti* (modification of the mind-stuff).[2] This "mind-object contact" is necessary for knowledge to arise. In this way the Advaita Vedānta epistemology of Gauḍapāda exhibits a form of "soft realism" in that the nature of the phenomenal world and physical perception is acknowledged and given some status.

But, from *paramārtha* or the perspective of the highest truth, this cannot be entirely accepted. For everything except the Self is only an illusory appearance caused by nescience or ignorance. From this perspective, then, the nature and status of the external object and physical perception is devalued. Objects are seen to be dependent upon the experiencer and vice versa. Objects "exist" or last only as long as the perceiver perceives them. Beyond this recognition and time duration they cease to "exist." So also is the case with subjective ideas or experiences.[3] In this way the whole world of perceived duality is called an "act of the mind" or the mind's "imagination."[4] It is because of the modifications of the mind (*citta-vṛttis*) that the external world appears as dual.[5]

---

1. *MK* II. 14; III. 29-31; IV. 24, 25, 61, 62 and 87.

2. "Perception requires a modification (*vṛtti*) of the mind, a change, so to speak, in its proper form after the form of the object; it requires an illumination of the object by the light of consciousness . . . the self, in that state of consciousness wherein perceptual experience takes place, is always involved with the world. To be awake means to be caught-up with forms and relations; it means to have the mind filled with objects and with desires generated by its contact with these objects. Perceptual experience not only illuminates an outer world *to* consciousness but also brings the changing world *into* consciousness; it involves the self and the world." Deutsch, *op. cit.*, pp. 91-2.

3. *MK* II. 14, 15; III. 24-26; IV. 72. etc.

4. This aspect of Gauḍapāda's meta-psychology will be dealt with in the next section.

5. *MK* IV. 72.

For all practical purposes the Self perceives the external world through the instrumentality of the mind. The mind, as it were, forms the liaison between the Self on the one hand, and the object on the other. But from the standpoint of the Self, both the mind and the objects of the mind are mere illusions. Thus any form of this dual relationship is said to be mere appearance and thus likened to "imagination."

The arguments which Gauḍapāda uses in his explanation are reminiscent of Buddhist Vijñānavāda theory. But he is not a "subjective idealist." Rather, he is an "Absolute Idealist" in that he posits a basis for all experience. Consciousness alone is real, it has no beginning nor end. It alone is the substratum of all knowledge.[1]

From what has been indicated, Gauḍapāda uses the term *manas* which suggests two meanings upon which he plays to indicate the nature of the Self and the method of release or realization. The first meaning again is that of the "empirical mind". The other and truer meaning is that of "Mind" or "Consciousness" which is the higher Self (*Ātman*). This is the key to the many paradoxical statements both in Gauḍapāda's text and in the Advaita tradition. Gauḍapāda dwells on this latter aspect in his rather rigorous non-dualism. The knowledge of the empirical mind and its workings are self-evident. But the real nature of the "mind" as "Mind" is hidden or veiled from the individual. So it is upon this aspect, the goal of Advaita, which he dwells consistently.

Besides the use of the terms *jiva* (living being), *draṣṭṛ* (seer), and *grāhaka* (cognizer) for the subject or witness of experience, Gauḍapāda also uses the terms *manas*, *citta*, and *vijñāna* synonymously for the Mind. The Mind or Consciousness is

---

1. *MK* IV. 26-28, 47-52, 72, 77, 79-81. Gauḍapāda often appears to walk the thin line between subjective idealism and monistic idealism. That he is not a solipsist is evident from his refutation of the subjective idealist position and his adamant non-dual stand. The subject and object are both included in his idealism and find their substratum in Pure Consciousness. He often appears as a subjectivist due to his thorough-going idealism wherein he talks from the *paramārtha* perspective. Thus he says that the mind is an "appearance" of consciousness, that the reality and existence of anything is relative to the mind which experiences it, and so forth.

considered to be unborn, non-dual, immovable, immaterial and all-pervading, and yet it appears as dual, moving, and as an object.[1] As the pure essence of Consciousness, it is described negatively as *asvapna* and *anidrā* (without spiritual sleep or delusion),[2] *anābhāsa* (not appearing or manifesting in the form of objects),[3] *asaṅga* (having no attachment or relation to any thing),[4] *amanībhāva* (when the empirical mind ceases to exist),[5] and somewhat positively as *sanirvāṇa* (with cessation or freedom).[6]

Thus, the *manas* or *citta* as Consciousness is entirely different from anything else. It is unique. It is not a product nor a collocation of conditions, nor is it further reducible into any constituents. It is foundational, the ground or substratum of all else. It is neither an attribute of something, nor possessed by anything. It does not come under any category of substance, attribute or action. For it is the basis of all. Consciousness is said to be eternal, unproduced, infinite, unlimited and self-revealing. It is undifferentiated, distinctionless unity, remaining ever unaffected and unchanged. That Consciousness is the presupposition of all knowledge and of the threefold division of subject-object relationship. It alone exists being One and Non-dual.[7]

In conclusion, Gauḍapāda follows the Upaniṣadic tradition concerning the nature of man as a spiritual and psychophysical entity. As a thoroughgoing Advaitin he negates all duality and ultimately posits the Self (*Ātman*) which is non-different from *Brahman* or *Turīya*, as the highest, pure, non-dual Mind or Consciousness. A good summation which reflects Gauḍapāda's position suggests that,

---

1. *MK* IV. 45 in particular.
2. *MK* I. 16; IV. 36; IV. 81.
3. *MK* III. 46.
4. *MK* III. 45, IV. 72, 79 and 96.
5. *MK* III. 31.
6. *MK* III. 37.
7. A good account of this subject is found in S.K. Saksena, *Nature of Consciousness in Hindu Philosophy* (Delhi : Motilal Banarsidass, 1971). A relevant summary is given on pages 60-1, 102-3, and 132-140.

The Vedāntic view, in particular the Advaitic view, is that *antaḥkaraṇa* or the mind, is like everything, a product of *māyā*. The self alone is consciousness, and consciousness cannot arise as a contingent factor of subject-object relation. The Advaitin agrees with the modern psychologists and says that mind is just a totality of conscious states and processes. The self which is neither mind nor matter is the ground of both mental and physical states of existences. That which reveals everything, viz., consciousness, is the basis of all experiences whether it is psychic or physical. That mind is not consciousness is established on an analysis of the three states of experience, viz., the waking, dreaming and sleeping experiences. Consciousness is not mere knowing, it involves transcendence of the objects known and the knowing process. Mind is that which has a locus in time and space, whereas consciousness is that which is not limited either by time or space, but still is that which gives a meaning to these. Mind, like matter, is only an appearance of consciousness. Just as in dreams the material substantive experience of waking life becomes only an appearance, so also in the light of pure consciousness the mental and physical experiences merely become illusions.[1]

3. Gauḍapāda's Theory of Mind Creation

This duality, possessed of subject and object, is a mere vibration of Consciousness. And Consciousness is objectless; hence It is declared to be eternally without relations.
—*MK* IV. 72

As earlier indicated, Gauḍapāda relates four agencies responsible for the manifestation of the world appearance.[2] The Self, God, *Māyā*, and the Mind are the four given.[3] These are shown to be not four different possibilities but rather one process as seen from differing perspectives.

1. Sarasvati Chennakesavan, *The Concept of Mind in Indian Philosophy* (Bombay : Asia Publishing House, 1960), pp. viii-ix.
2. See Chapter IV section 3.
3. *MK* II. 12, III. 19, IV. 72 and III. 31.

That these are all essentially non-different is due to their similarity concerning the manifestation of the phenomenal universe upon a substratum which in this case is pure Consciousness. The Self (*ātman*) is not different from *Brahman* or *Turīya*, nor is the Lord (as the lower form or manifestation of *Brahman*) essentially different from the higher form, nor is the Mind different from this non-dual substrate Consciousness. Even *māyā* is related to these lofty principles on the basis of its process of differentiation or manifestation on a substratum.

The key to these agencies is their mode of manifestation. This is expressed metaphorically with the images of :

1. the process of imagination (*kalpana*),[1]
2. the "creation" of an appearance or illusion through supernatural or magical means (*māyā*),[2]
3. the vibration, movement, or oscillations of consciousness (*citta-spandita*),[3]
4. something dependent on the immediate perception of the mind for its "existence" (*mano-dṛśya*),[4]
5. turning the mind outward thereby "creating" through "imagination" what pre-exists or subsists within the Mind.[5]

These images share some common features. First, the nature or reality of phenomenal universe is questioned. It is said to exist but its persistence or ultimate validity is denied. A higher or truer status is given to that which "manifests" the lesser one This ground or substratum is the second common feature. It is that pure non-dual Consciousness however it be expressed as *Brahman*, as God, etc. Thirdly, and most important here is the basic characteristic of the processes of the mind used in these images. For the characteristics of perception, imagination, conceptualization, and so forth are essential processes within each person. Through the use of this terminology and the picture which is thus created, Gauḍapāda easily suggests the

1. *MK*. II. 12-16.
2. *MK* II. 12, III. 10, 19, 23, 24, 27, IV. 57-58, etc.
3. *MK* III. 28, IV. 72.
4. *MK* III. 31, IV. 63-66.
5. *MK* II. 13.

process of world generation and the consequent phenomenal manifestation. To an aspirant undergoing the experiential practice of meditation, this image is a familiar one. For the first result of this practice is the knowledge of the mind and its workings, not theoretically but experientially. In this way the examples are very concrete and easily understandable by the practitioner of meditation. Further, they are a part of his meditational process as the aspirant personally partakes in this inner process.

Once again Gauḍapāda uses the terms *manas* and *citta* in the double sense of the "individual empirical mind" as well as the "cosmic Mind" which is pure non-dual Consciousness. The Mind or Consciousness is also called the "unborn" mind and the "non-mind" (*amanībhāva*).[1] What he suggests by this is that the process of world-creation is due to the activity or the processes of the "mind" in its empirical sense and that when this process ceases or subsides, the true nature of pure non-dual Consciousness, which though present at all times, is experienced, or rather it simply "is".[2]

The process herein is described as the "Mind" or "mind" (*manas*, *citta*, or *vijñāna*) moving, oscillating or vibrating (*spandita*).[3] When it does so an illusion of an objective existence or an appearance of objects is produced. To fully illustrate this image, Gauḍapāda uses the analogy of the fire-brand (alāta).[4] For the "whirling" movement of the fire-brand "creates" different forms, shapes and patterns. When it is not in motion, it is seen to be free from all appearances and remains changeless. The straight and crooked lines and patterns created from the one point are likened to the creation of any and all names (*samākhyā* or *nāma*) and forms (*rūpa*) in the phenomenal universe. This movement of the single pointed fire-brand creating plural forms is also similar to the process of the Consciousness "creating," as it were, the duality of the perceiver and perceived. This helps to explain the paradoxical and impossible idea of the

1. *MK* III. 31 and IV. 28.
2. *MK* III. 31-32.
3. *MK* III. 28, IV. 47 and 72.
4. *MK* IV. 47-52.

seeming change in the unchanging substratum. As the fire-brand/consciousness moves, the variegated names and forms constituting the world are perceived! When the mind/fire-brand is still, the vibrations cease and all the shapes "merge" or disappear, as it were, into the single-pointedness of the substratum.

Further, the forms or appearances when the fire-brand is in motion are related only to it and have no other source. The appearances stay at the tip of the fire-brand when motionless and do not go elsewhere. They do not enter the fire-brand, nor did they really emerge from the fire-brand. The appearances neither go out of, nor enter into the fire-brand. Similar is the manifestation of non-dual Consciousness into the plural world. The manifold plurality is neither identical with, nor independent from *Ātman* or Consciousness. It is neither separate nor non-separate from it. The pluralistic universe is nothing but this Reality, yet the world is not "real". Reality is not the world, yet the multiple universe has no existence without this Reality underlying it.[1]

In this way, the generation of the world of duality and also the essential non-dual nature of everything is explained. Gauḍapāda realizes that it is difficult and ultimately impossible to give a complete intellectual explanation for the how and the why of this process. For the truth of non-duality is always beyond intellectual comprehension as it is not subject to the dualistic sub-structure of our language and thought processes and transcends these at all times.

Thus the Advaitin declares that "the world exists only in the mind"[2] and that it is only "the movement of consciousness producing the appearance of the perceiver and the perceived" thereby "imagining variety where it is not."[3] The world is said to be really only the objectivization of the mind imposed on the Absolute *Ātman*. This is also expressed in other ways. Imagination or creation is also called "projection" or "super-imposition". One use of the term *māyā* by Gauḍapāda is in

1. *MK* II. 33-35.
2. *MK* IV. 45-48, 72, 77 and I. 17. Cp. *Bṛh. Up.* I. 53 : "All this is truly mind" (*sarvaṃ mana eva*).
3. *MK* II. 15, 17 and IV. 47.

reference to this process.[1] The Self, through *māyā*, posits the internal and external contents. It is the non-moving or unchanging Mind which moves on account of *māyā*. It is literally a super-imposition on the non-dual *Brahman*. The pure Consciousness or *Ātman* deludes Itself by Itself, projects (*kaplana*) the pluralistic universe which is nothing but Itself, and cognizes (*budhyate*) the objects so created.[2]

To illustrate this Gauḍapāda uses the well-known rope-snake analogy. The rope substratum projects (*vikalpa*) various names and forms. It can be misperceived as a snake, a piece of stick, a streak of water, a crack in the ground and so forth. When the real nature of it is discovered the illusions disappear. In a similar fashion is *Ātman* misperceived.

This process of *vikalpa* or *kalpana* suggests a misconception or false ascription. It is a fiction or construction of the mind whereby subjective categories not of *a priori* origin are superimposed upon the one undifferentiated being (*sat* or *Brahman*) or Consciousness (*cit*). Space, time and causality, for example, are such categories of the mind and are said to be constructions of the intellect for the purpose of understanding. As such they convert indeterminate perception, experience, or knowledge into a coherent order of intelligible experience. They have validity only within the limits of our empirical knowledge.

From the *paramārtha* perspective they are merely illusive conceptual constructions, merely names or words having no real objects for their signification, or unreal forms of ideal construction. For when the individual has the direct intuitive apprehension of *Brahman*, he transcends the limits of empirical knowledge. In short, the conceptual constructions are not the framework of the real but only those of mind-imposed structure on Reality. This superimposition is essentially that of the

1. *MK* I. 16 (*anādi māyayā*), II. 31 (*svapna māye*), II. 19 (*devasya māyā*), III. 19 (*māyayā bhidyate*), III. 29 (*māyayā spandate manaḥ*), IV. 58 (*janma māyopamam, yathā māyāmayāt*), III. 27 (*māyayā jāta*), III. 24 (*māyayā jāyate*), IV. 69 (*māyāmayo jīvaḥ*).

2. *MK* II. 12. cp. "The statement that the world is born of *Ātman* simply means that it is a superimposition on *Ātman*." Swāmī Satchidanandendra Saraswati, *Salient Features of Śaṅkara's Vedānta* (Holenarsipur : Adhyatma Prakasha Karyalaya, 1967), p. 123.

subject-object relation of determinate perception.[1] This is the classic imposition of the *dvandvas*, the pairs of opposites, upon non-dual Consciousness or Reality. The impositions of subject and object, being and non-being, the one and the many, finite and infinite, individuality and universality, liberation and bondage, and so forth are but concepts of the mind which are taken for granted and agreed upon conventionally. It is granted that these are the basis of ordinary experience, but the point is that the individual is deceived or deluded by them and by erroneously identifying with them and giving them a falsely ultimate status, the individual suffers frustration, anxiety, grief and misery in his daily life in the world. For Advaita says that this is not the true nature of existence or reality. The nature of the *Ātman*, Mind, or Consciousness is really *asaṅga*, never in touch with any object, unattached, and ever without relations. Thus, though the multiple phenomena manifest upon it, as it were, this non-dual principle remains unaffected in every way.

This is further illustrated by Gauḍapāda in his arguments concerning the idea of the state of waking being as unreal or illusory as that of the dream state.[2] The crux of the argument relevant here centers again on the nature of the subject-object relationship, that these are interdependent and determine one another.[3] Further, this "perceiver-perceived" relation is really only that which is "presented" to consciousness in both states. And as the dream state is seen to be illusory and but the product of the mind when compared with the waking state, so also the waking state is likewise illusory and mind-dependent on the basis of its comparison and subsequent sublation from the perspective of the non-dualistic state of deep sleep and *Turiya*, and

1. *MK* III. 29-31, IV. 61-62, 72, 87-88.
2. *MK* III. 29-31, IV. 61-62, 65-68.
3. "*Citta* (the mind) manifests itself in the form of duality as much in the waking state as in dream . . . the phenomena noticed . . . are not independent of the mind there; nor is that mind independent of the . . . observer. The phenomena there do not enjoy an existence of their own apart from the mind noticing them ; nor has the mind any existence of its own independent of the waking observer. Apart from the witnessing Self neither the mind nor the phenomena enjoy any absolute existence, for they are relative to each

the latter in particular.[1]

Duality is thus said to be perceived only by the mind. But when it becomes "non-mind" and the functions of thinking (*manana*) in the sense of *vikalpa* or *kalpana* cease, there is no more duality. That in the absence of the "mind," the pluralistic universe totally disappears from experience is the argument given for the belief that the world is but a perception or "creation" of the mind.

Gauḍapāda does not recognize duality in any form as being ultimately real, though it exists and is the basic infrastructure of our relations within the world of everyday experience. All dualistic conceptions based on the subject and object relation or the opposition of extremes such as being and non-being, are the work of the discriminating mind. This process, variously called *citta spandita, kalpana, vikalpa* and *māyā*, transforms in thought through images and conceptions the perception of reality as it really is not. Behind this imposed dualistic structure lies Reality, pure and non-dual. The so-called manifold universe is thus called a "projection of the mind" temporarily appearing as dual. But the analysis of experience indicates experientially the unity of our experience in the three states as due to this underlying unity of Consciousness. What Gauḍapāda denies is simply the "independence" of the

---

other .... Everything there is really the mind, and the mind really Ātman .... Waking and dream are each the result of mind-vibration peculiar to the respective states." Swami Satchidanandendra Saraswati, *op. cit.*, pp. 74-6.

1. There are important differences between the state of deep sleep and *Turīya* which are fundamental to Gauḍapāda's system of thought and practice. See *MK* I.12-15 and III. 34-36. Gauḍapāda is careful not to confuse "the fourth" with the "causal state" of deep sleep as could be interpreted from the descriptions of *samādhi* given in Yoga and Vedānta texts. They are similar in that non-duality, i.e., the non-perception of duality is a common characteristic. The difference is that *Prājña* is the objectless world of sleep, while *Turīya* is the "sleepless" world of Reality. As such the state of deep sleep is still enmeshed in ignorance though it remains latent therein until re-manifestation takes place. It is the doorway or causal "state" of dual experience and in relation to the other states of experience. But *Turīya* is neither a "state" of experience nor a condition of "unconsciousness." Rather it is the non-dual, changeless and pure consciousness which underlies the three states. The attainment of this state is said to be true and everlasting freedom versus the temporary and unconscious state of deep sleep-like states.

objects from the mind and its structures as well as their eternality. His work is basically, then, an attempt to show the illusory or unreal nature of the phenomenal world by bringing out the antinomies of empirical relations and to emphasize that the ultimate and true reality can be only that which is free from these.

4. Soteriological Aspects of Gauḍapāda's Meta-psychology

> When, (following the instruction of scriptures and the teacher), the mind ceases to think as a consequence of the realisation of the Truth that is the Self, then the mind attains the state of not being the mind; in the absence of things to be perceived, it becomes a non-perceiver.
>
> -*MK*, III. 32

Gauḍapāda's phenomenological analysis and meta-psychology reveal the soteriological theory upon which his advocated practices, especially meditation, are based.

One use of the term *māyā* is in reference to the condition of spiritual sleep or ignorance of true Reality.[1] Man, enmeshed in *māyā*, in the illusoriness or deceptiveness of the world, participating in the binding processes of "mind creation," and its dualistic framework, is said to be spiritually asleep (*nidrā*).[2] For real wakefulness is spiritual awakening (*prabodha*).[3]

There are two aspects of this state of ignorance or spiritual sleep. First, the states of waking and dream are collectively called *svapna* (dream) wherein reality is "misapprehended" (*anyathā-grahaṇa*) as the variegated world of plurality. This error or wrong cognition is termed *vikṣepa* (projection) in later Advaita. The second aspect of this state of nescience is called *nidrā* (sleep) itself and refers to the "non-apprehension" of Reality (*tattvājñāna*). This was later termed *āvaraṇa*, the veiling, covering or concealing aspect of primordial ignorance.[4] This beginningless ignorance (*anādi māyā*) is equated with the lack of "knowledge" (*jñāna*)

1. *MK* I. 16.
2. *MK* I. 14 and 15.
3. *MK* I. 16.
4. *MK* I. 16. Gauḍapāda also uses the term *āvaraṇa* in *MK* IV. 82-84 and 97.

of Reality. This non-knowing (ajñāna) or non-apprehension (*nidrā*) is said to be the cause (*kāraṇa*) and misapprehension is the effect (*kārya*).

Gauḍapāda also uses other meta-psychological terms for this basic ignorance. The terms *mithyā* (false due to being erroneously cognized), *kalpita* (wrongly imagined), *viparyāsa* or *viparyaya* (error or delusion in the sense of taking what is unreal or false to be real or true)[1] are used synonymously with *nidrā*, *svapna* and *māyā*. These describe man's spiritual situation in the world. They are intellectual concepts which collectively express man's estrangement from Reality. The terms are used figuratively for their spiritual significance. They indicate that the crux of man's spiritual problem is erroneous knowledge. Mis-apprehension and non-apprehension continue until the situation is rectified by the onset of true or right knowledge. Gauḍapāda declares :

> When the individual, sleeping under the influence of beginningless *Māyā*, is awakened, then he realises the birthless, sleepless, dreamless, non-dual (*Turiya*).[2]

The basic spiritual dilemma for man, then, is his false perception of reality and the consequent erroneous identification with the modes of perception through which consciousness expresses itself. Also, the impressions of the duality, its common-sensuality, is so deeply rooted in the psychological make-up of the individual that it is not easy to understand, perceive and realize the non-dual Reality which is the substrate of this manifold appearance. Perceiving through the vehicles of the senses and the mind and identifying with them, the individual is thus blinded to the perception of the true nature of reality. His mental agitations and disturbances do not allow him to realize or experience his real nature. They also cause the miseries and frustrations of life and deny man peace, happiness, etc.

Gauḍapāda suggests that this is in part due to the ease with which this process of superimposition, covering or concealment

---

1. *MK* IV. 41.
2. *MK* I. 16.

takes place.[1] Man naturally enmeshes himself in this web of primordial ignorance. Man's basic eagerness to grasp (*grahaṇa*) is also cited by Gauḍapāda as easily facilitating concealment. The false identification with the subject over against the objects of experience is the first part of man's bondage and consequent tribulations. The ego's possessiveness and attachment to objects completes the enslavement. The false belief in the separate reality of subject over object and the attraction towards object is said by Gauḍapāda to be the cause of *saṃsāra*, the cycle of transmigration and man's situation of suffering in the world.[2] Because of the ease with which this fundamental situation arises and its persistence, it is "uncovered" (*vivriyate*) with great difficulty.[3]

Gauḍapāda says that this notion of duality and its consequences for the individual arise from the mental pre-occupation with or obsession for the phenomenal appearance of duality. Owing to this persistent belief or faith in the reality of the unreal (*abhūtābhiniveśa*); the mind relentlessly proceeds in its outgoing activities. This is the concept of *māyā* at the personal level of individual participation rather than as an impersonal cosmic principle which merely affects the individual.[4] *Abhūtābhiniveśa* as the persistent belief in and fondness for duality is a congenital disposition conditioning all knowledge and thus makes the individual perceive plurality where there is really one, the non-dual pure Consciousness. As such it is the cause of bondage.

This mental pre-occupation and persistent belief in duality can be corrected according to Gauḍapāda. Using his example of causation, he suggests that the cause of causation is only the

1. *MK* IV. 82-84.
2. *MK* IV. 75 and 56.
3. *MK* IV. 82.
4. *MK* IV. 75 and 79. "If *avidyā* or nescience be interpreted as the root principle of all subjectivity and to work out its programme through a false belief in and attachment to the non-self and the subjective and the objective world constructed by it, then, it can be equated with Gauḍapāda's concept of *abhūtābhiniveśa*—the bliss and the predilection of the subject for the unreal plurality." from N. Tatia, *Studies in Jaina Philosophy* (Banaras : Jaina Cultural Research Society), pp. 120-1, quoted in E.A. Solomon's *Avidyā : A Problem of Truth and Reality*, (Ahmedabad, Gujarat University, 1969), pp. 209-210.

belief and obsession with that concept.[1] This is why he endeavours to point out the empty myth of causality which people in their delusory understanding maintain as true. By intellectually breaking down our faith in causality, the preceptor is, in effect, exploding the belief and faith in all of the familiar structures of the individual's world view. All concepts and categories imposed upon experience are challenged and through the various teaching methods of the *guru* are shown to be fallacious.

Speaking psychologically, Gauḍapāda suggests that *abhūtābhiniveśa* is the "out-going mind," the mind relating itself as possessive subject to its objects. When their absence is known, when duality disappears, the mind becomes unattached (*niḥsaṅga*) to them and "turns back" (*vinivartate*). This absence of relation to objects, the turning back and non-movement outwards is said to be the true state of the mind. As the unwavering, non-dual mind of pure experience it has become the unattached, unborn Consciousness.[2] This is the state of *amanībhāva* (non-mind) of Gauḍapāda's meta-psychology. It is the state of quiescence, peace, bliss--the state of Self-realization described from the perspective of the individual's mind processes.

This "non-mind" (*amanībhāva*) condition is the *samādhi* of the *yogins* wherein the mind is controlled and laid to rest (i.e., as in *amanastā* or *nigrhita manas*).[3] When the "mind" becomes "non-mind" it becomes free from the three states and their determinations (*vikalpa*) and is said to be identical with *Brahman, Turīya,* or Pure Consciousness.[4] The individual ceases to imagine or

1. *MK* IV. 56.
2. *MK* IV. 79-80.
3. *MK* III. 32, 34 and 37.
4. "The *ātman* is not a mere aggregate of consciousness as is sometimes assumed by the Buddhists and other allied schools of thought, and this can only be proved by a reference to the state of sleep, when through a natural process the incessant flow of thought is brought to a stop and yet the light of consciousness is not extinguished or put out. And once this is proved, one must try to realize it consciously and with its conscious realization the necessity for leaving one state of consciousness and entering into another undifferentiated state of apparent consciousness ceases altogether. Then one feels the independence of the *Ātman* even while awake to the numerous states of thought or consciousness. There is no further necessity of contracting the thoughts once this absolute freedom of the *ātman* is realized,

think dualistically (*saṅkalpa*) and thus is said to be free from cognition due to the lack of objects to grasp. The subject-object distinction disappears on the realization of Truth.[1] Positively stated, the empirical mind reaches the condition of quietude or equipoise (*sāmya*) when it becomes unified or one with the Absolute Mind.[2] Rather than engaging in the processes of "mind creation," the mind is said to desist from all activity and remains in its birthless, non-dual, motionless nature as Mind or Pure Consciousnesss.[3]

How is this accomplished? Gauḍapāda uses the phrases "outgoing" and then "turning back" for the movement of consciousness. The process here is described in negative terms. On the

---

for the *ātman* neither contracts nor expands. It is only the mind that possesses this twin aspect of contraction and expansion, and the *ātman* being in close identification with it, appears to be contracting and expanding. Hence it seems, at one time, withdrawing itself and again coming out and spreading itself all around, as the mind goes to rest and again becomes active. There is no withdrawal on the part of the *ātman*, for it is everywhere and all the time the same identical reality, without any contraction or expansion whatsoever in itself. Hence it must be carefully remembered that only because, in the waking state, it becomes impossible to have any idea of the *ātman* in its purity, free trom identification with the states of consciousness, one is taken to the state of sleep (the reference here is to the *Bṛhadāraṇyaka Upaniṣad* whereas the reference in the *Māṇḍūkya* is to *Turīya*), where through a natural process the states of consciousness cease and it becomes easy to get hold of *ātman* as it is per se . . . . As one must pass beyond the state of waking . . . are equally states of mind, and the *Ātman* is not a state but an unchanging entity which remains the same in all states and conditions." Govindagopal Mukhopadhyaya, *Studies in the Upanishads* (Calcutta : Sanskrit College, 1960) pp. 232-233.

1. "The mind though its own nature is undoubtedly without the two (i.e., the percipient and the perceptible), yet it moves owing to illusion with the appearance of the two (*MK* III. 30, IV. 62). This duality compromising the movable and the unmovable is therefore perceptible only by the mind. Hence when the mind becomes non-mind, i.e., when it ceases from its function of thinking, no duality is experienced (III. 31). The cessation of the function of thinking of the mind, or, in other words, the state of non-mind is reached when the mind through its knowledge of the truth of the *Ātman* does not think anything being non-congnizant owing to the absence of the things to be cognized (III. 32)." Bhattacharya, *op. cit.*, p. cxxx.

2. *MK* IV. 80.

3. *MK* IV. 80-81.

one hand, it is called a process of "reversing" the extroversion of consciousness. Liberation is achieved through the process of introversion, going from the external and internal world of objects (i.e., duality) to the state of Self-awareness (non-duality). On the other hand, the problem is one of erroneous knowledge (*ajñāna*, *svapna*, *nidrā*, *māyā*, etc.) and its "removal" leads to freedom. As the rope is discovered by "negating" the appearance of the snake, the Self is to be realized by "removing" what is illusorily superimposed upon it. The "re-discovery," "realization," or "knowledge of" reality "as it really is" is the goal, the only antidote to man's painful worldly situation.

The processes of "reversal" and "removal" refer to the new condition, experience or knowledge which results from the negation of that which causes bondage and its consequent suffering. For in that new spiritual experience all that the individual previously knew is transformed. It is said that upon this realization or epistemological change, the individual is never again subject to false knowledge or any misapprehension of Reality.[1] The transformation is there and language tries to express this new condition but only indicates a semblance of that direct intuitive experience. And that is voiced mostly in terms which negate qualities of common or normal everyday experience and the processes involved therein.

In conclusion then, Gauḍapāda describes this total process psychologically both to explain the theoretical aspect of his teachings and to describe the process which the individual aspirant goes through during the culmination of the practice of meditation. For this Gauḍapāda teaches the enquiry into and the analysis of experience, the nature of the mind, and finally, the methods by which it can be mastered.

1. *MK* IV. 47.

CHAPTER VI

THE SOTERIOLOGY OF GAUḌAPĀDA'S *MĀṆḌŪKYA KĀRIKĀ*

I bow down to that *Yoga* that is well known as free from relationships, joyful to all beings, beneficial, free from dispute, non-contradictory, and set forth in the scriptures.
—*MK* IV. 2

As an *upadeśa-śāstra* (a practical teaching text), the *Māṇḍūkya Kārikā* is primarily concerned with the question of liberation (*mokṣa*).[1] Gauḍapāda's metaphysics, epistemology, psychology and practical spiritual disciplines all relate to this essential soteriological concern of Advaita.[2] His text assumes this problem

1. The major soteriological verses comprise approximately one-third of the total text although the text as a whole can be said to be an *upadeśa-śāstra*. The major verses comprising this essential concern are as follows : MK I.2, 5, 10, 15, 16, 19-23, 24-25, 27-28, 29; II. 32, 34, 35, 38; III. 1, 4, 5, 8, 9, 10, 14-16, 29-48; IV. 2, 30, 42-43, 46, 52, 54, 55-56, 60, 72-99. The esssential verses describing the meditative discipline and its background are given in full in Appendix I. These are drawn from the principal *upādeśa* portion which comes at the end of the third *prakaraṇa* of the *Māṇḍūkya Kārikā*.

2. "For India, truth is not precious in itself; it becomes precious by virtue of its soteriological function, because knowledge of truth helps man to liberate himself. It is not the possession of truth that is the supreme end of the Indian sage: it is liberation, and conquest of absolute freedom." (p. 4). "In India metaphysical knowledge always has a soteriological purpose. Thus only metaphysical knowledge (*vidyā, jñāna, prajñā*)—that is, the knowledge of ultimate realities—is valued and sought, for it alone procures liberation. For it is by "knowledge" that man, casting off the illusions of the world of phenomena, "awakens". By knowledge—and that means: by practicing withdrawal, the effect of which will be to make him find his own

of human life giving the details of bondage and the promise of liberation, setting forth the nature of man's situation and the corrective procedures for this, as well as outlining the nature of the state of liberation to be attained. This is the religious or spiritual purpose of the text, for it was written by a spiritual preceptor (*guru*) for aspirants (*sādhakas*) seeking liberation from the round of *saṃsāra* and freedom in this very life.

1. Man's Religious Situation : The Problem of Bondage and Mokṣa as The Goal of Life

> There is in evidence a (mere) craving for false objects, (though) no duality is in existence there. Realising the non-existence of duality, one becomes free from craving for false things, and one does not undergo birth.
> —MK IV. 75

> No soul ever came under any veil. They are by nature pure as well as illumined and free from the very beginning. Thus being endowed with the power (of knowledge), they are said to know.
> —*MK* IV. 98

Gauḍapāda's *Māṇḍūkya Kārikā* assumes the Advaita Vedānta view of man's existential spiritual situation. It presupposes two existential possibilities for man, that of the state of *duḥkha* (bondage) and that of *mokṣa* (freedom). The Advaitin thus sees two types of existence, authentic and inauthentic. This is in sharp contrast with those who hold that man's finite everyday situation is not only the real situation but also an authentic one. Man's situation is said by Advaita to be a state of bondage, fraught with pain, frustration, anxiety and misery. That *duḥkha* or suffering is the state of normal man is put forth on the basis of the realizability of the condition of *mokṣa* which is liberation, freedom or authentic existence.

---

center, to make him coincide with his "true spirit" (*puruṣa, ātman*). Knowledge is transformed into a kind of meditation, and metaphysics becomes soteriology. In India not even "logic" is without a soteriological function in its beginnings. (p. 13). Mircea Eliade, *Yoga : Immortality and Freedom* (Princeton : Princeton University Press, 1958).

Suffering is said to constitute the very structure of man's temporal existence. Man's participation within the world upon enquiry reveals its duplicity. Conditioned by, participating within, and buffeted by pairs of opposites, such as pleasure and pain, man rarely reflects on the nature of his life. Holding onto pleasures, endeavouring to forget the suffering in life, distracting himself from the problems, anxieties, frustration and pain of his worldly life, man tries to make the best of his situation and seeks to alleviate this frustration But *duḥkha* is said to be the basic fact of life. It symbolizes the ambiguous character of life and the self-contradictory nature of man. As a concept it points to man's finitude and all of its ramifications such as his subjection to *karma* (retributive action), time, death and so forth. The awareness of this situation constrains man to reflect and enquire into the nature of his and the world's existence. It points to another state of existence free from suffering, finitude and death, that of *mokṣa*. It awakens man to his human dilemma and puts him on the quest of truth and freedom to rectify this inauthenticity and alienation from a true and complete life. So begins the pursuit of *mokṣa* based on the knowledge of its possibility.

Duḥkha thus represents man's essential unawareness of the depth of his own existence. Man's involvement in ignorance and illusion and his subjection to the processes of life make him forgetful of his real existence as the Self (*ātman*). Falsely identifying himself with the body-mind complex he becomes alienated from his true state. The conscious identification of the Self with its adjuncts creates a condition of individuality, separateness or insularity and thus the *jīva* lives a "limited" rather than a "complete" life.

This state of bondage or suffering (*duḥkha*) is designated *saṃsāra* by Gauḍapāda. It is the condition of cause and effect, the repetition of birth and death, the participation in the world of *māyā* both in the external world of phenomena and also personally on an ego level. The belief (*abhiniveśa*) in the dualistic process, the attachment (*saṅga*) to objects, and the identification with the body-mind complex are said to be the cause of this process.[1] This is the basic "ignorance" of one's real

1. *MK* IV. 10, 75, 91-94.

nature. Man's not knowing true reality (*tattvājñāna*) and his egotistical participation in the unreal world of *māyā* is the reason for his bondage.[1]

The removal of this basic falsehood is the remedy to man's plight. As "ignorance" is the cause, it must be eradicated. And when the false belief, perception or understanding of reality is destroyed through knowledge (*jñāna*), *saṃsāra* is removed or rather disappears.[2] As attachment etc. is responsible for the wanderings in *saṃsāra*, the individual becomes non-attached through knowledge. He "turns back" from the false pursuit of the non-real and reaches the non-dual Reality.[3] This is accomplished by the realization of the Self (*ātmasatyānubodha*), which is the sole reality.[4] With the realization of this truth the individual attains to *mokṣa* which is release or freedom from sorrow, desire, fear, etc.

Mokṣa, then, refers to the attainment of spiritual freedom and the individual's release from the trammels and fetters of life. This condition is given supreme valuation by Gauḍapāda and by Advaita Vedānta as a whole. Faced with the acuteness of suffering and bondage the individual seeks relief. Finding that normal life is inauthentic and essentially one of alienation from

---

1. This appears at first sight to be a classical doublebind situation. The argument is circular in that it suggests that man is in bondage due to ignorance and in ignorance because of his bound condition. But what it is really attempts to communicate is quite different. The beginning or ultimate cause of this situation is not and cannot be known and the pursuit of it is useless as it remains an unanswerable question. The point is that each man is born into this situation unawares and it is perpetuated by his willing, though often, unconscious participation in it. Though it is beginningless, it does have an end. This is the promise of release or liberation through the realization of the truth of Reality.

2. *MK* IV. 56. Śaṅkara in his introduction to the Upaniṣadic commentary states that "Just as the normal state of a man afflicted by disease, consists in his getting cured of the disease, similarly the normal state of the Self, stricken with identification with misery, is regained through the cessation of the phenomenal universe of duality. The end in view is the realization of non-duality. Since the phenomenal world of duality is a creation of ignorance, it can be eradicated through knowledge."

3. *MK* IV.78-80.

4. *MK* III. 32.

one's true nature or reality, the individual begins the pursuit of this ideal. Though to the bound man it is merely an ideal and an aim at first, the tradition of those who have found such a release and liberation, and who live authentically in this freedom, happiness and peace is the external evidence of what the individual must prove existentially for himself.

Mokṣa is thus a state or condition of "freedom."[1] This "freedom" is usually defined negatively as a freedom "from" suffering, bondage and all that that implies for the individual. On the positive side, *mokṣa* as that which is ultimately valuable is defined as freedom "to" be authentic and to live life fully and completely without delusion and restriction. This is a condition of life, of the "here-and-now," and is not the redemption of an after-death state. It is a new condition of being, the realization of one's real nature, the ever-free Self. It is the discovery of what one always was, the direct personal intuitive experience of one's inmost depths of being. It is an epistemological change affecting both the individual and his relation to the world. For *mokṣa* is *Brahma-vidyā*, the knowledge or direct perception of Reality. It is not the dissolution of the world per se, but only the disappearance of a false outlook. Freedom consists in the dissolution of all empirical categories and the subject-object distinction. The world of experience with its distinctions is said to disappear,as it were, for the individual who recognizes the non-dual oneness of *Brahman* and *Ātman*.[2]

As the snake is sublated through knowledge revealing the rope, so also is the case of the superimposition of the manifold world upon *Brahman* being removed through knowledge (*jñāna* or *anubhava*). It is not the "production" of anything but rather a "re-discovery." Nor can it be categorized as a modification, purification, refinement, attainment or acquisition of anything. It is not even a change of state, a separation from Nature, nor union with *Brahman*, nor the *jiva* going to *Brahman* or vice versa.

---

1. For a brief but excellent discussion of this basic concept of freedom in Indian philosophy see Karl H. Potter, *Presuppositions of India's Philosophies* (Englewood Cliffs, N.J. Prentice-Hall Inc., 1963), pp. 1-24 and 48-49 in perticular.

2. *MK* III. 32-33 and 37-38.

Mokṣa is nothing but being established in one's real Self. It is the knowledge that *Brahman* is the only ultimate Reality, that the *jiva* is non-different from *Brahman*, and that the world of plurality and multiplicity is false or delusory, because it is a superimposition on *Brahman*. What is called release, then, is really only the attainment of what is already there. Positively, it is said to be the discovery of the Self (*ātman*) and negatively this knowledge or realization is said to be simply the removal of ignorance concerning reality. This new outlook affects both the individual's understanding of himself and also of his relation to the world.

Gauḍapāda also reminds the aspirant that this talk of bondage and liberation is from the standpoint of the relative.[1] While the falsity of bondage can only be stated from the *paramārtha* perspective or experience, from this standpoint there is only the ever-liberated Self. The Self never really becomes bound and so there is no real question of its bondage and the need to attain release at any particular point in time. For the Self is of the nature of eternal release. It is freedom itself. The highest truth is that there it neither *saṃsāra* nor *mokṣa*. When the obscuration by *māyā* is removed through knowledge, release is said to be attained in a figurative sense only. Liberation thus signifies or represents the realization of what is ever-present, the eternal non-dual Reality, rather than the accomplishment of anything new. For the Absolute is not the fruit of activity as there is nothing to be done in reference to *Brahman*.[2] There is no cause of Self-Realization, for if it were an effect, it would be a perishable quantum and as finite as anything else. Only the removal of ignorance through knowledge, the direct personal intuitive experience of *Brahman*, is necessary to reveal what has always been there but veiled from immediate experience. Thus the path thereto is the *jñāna mārga*, the way of knowledge. Gauḍapāda defines this as *ātmasatyānubodha*, the realization of the truth of the Self. It is through the "unborn knowledge" that the "unborn Self" is realized.[3]

1. *MK* II. 32 and IV. 30 (also see Śaṅkara's commentary thereon).
2. *MK* III. 36.
3. *MK* III. 32-33.

2. Sādhanā or Spiritual Discipline

> Things to be rejected, realised, accepted, and made ineffective are to be known at the very beginning.
> —*MK* IV. 90

For the bound man to realize or actualize the condition of *mokṣa* in his life, he must undertake some process to initiate this change. This is called *sādhanā*, spiritual discipline. *Sādhanā* literally means "that by which something is performed," or more precisely, "the means to an end." In the spiritual quest, it refers to the essential preliminary discipline that leads to the attainment of the spiritual experience which is regarded as the *summum bonum*, the highest good, the *siddhi* (completion or perfection) of existence. *Sādhanā*, then, is the means or instrument by which *siddhi*, success or perfection, is attained.[1]

Sādhanā is thus a broad term which covers and contains anything which relates and is helpful to the realization of spiritual experience. It is the practical rather than the theoretical side of the religio-philosophical quest. As such it involves an attitude towards life as a whole and can best be described as the taking up of a new way of living. For it requires a radical change in attitude, direction and life-style. *Sādhanā* becomes a method or practice of living for the purpose of effecting spiritual change, growth and perfection.

Sādhanā combines the theoretical base with the practical preparation for Self-Realization. Philosophy and religion truly blend here. For, as was pointed out in a previous chapter, neither is really independent. They are interdependent and reciprocally related. Advaita Vedānta in general and Gauḍapāda in particular subscribe to this view of the goal of life being the achievement of *mokṣa* and all that this term implies. Everything becomes subsumed to that end. Philosophy is not for the sake of the intellect, nor is religion for anything other than this basic task or realization or enlightenment. They are both directed towards aiding the individual towards actualizing the *sādhya*, that which is to be obtained, which in this case is the *Brahman* or *Ātman* experience. Thus, only in the realm of thought

1. Brahma, *op. cit.*, p.13.

can this total attitude and way of life be categorized for the purpose of understanding. Metaphysics, epistemology, psychology, soteriology are all ultimately merely aspects of Vedāntic *sādhanā*. *Sādhanā* incorporates them all into a dynamic existential process of Self-discovery (*ātma-vidyā*).

As such Gauḍapāda gives the aspirant a basic and all-comprehensive *sādhanā*. Theory and practice are drawn from the illuminations of Self-realized individuals solely for the purpose of guiding seekers. This is said to be done out of compassion for the suffering, bound man. The *siddhas*, the perfected, enlightened or liberated beings, know of the difficulty in attaining *mokṣa*. As an ideal pursuit, Advaitic realization is not easily acquired due to basic ignorance.[1] Because of this, they saw the need for a process of education, of discipline, as preparation for Self-realization. Enlightenment requires the "attunement" of the whole being of the aspirant to enable him to become so transformed. Such a spiritual experience occurs only when the individual is fully prepared to receive such revelation or self-discovery. The *guru* gives the *sādhaka*, or practitioner of *sādhanā*, a total way of life consisting of the essence of the life philosophy, the goal to achieve, and the path of directions and procedural methods to pursue that end.

In *MK* IV. 90, Gauḍapāda gives a summary of his process of *sādhanā*. He says that four things are to be known by the aspirant at the beginning of the spiritual quest. These are to be worked with until the end or goal of liberation or Self-realization is achieved. First is that which is to be avoided or rejected (*heya*). Śaṅkara in his commentary says that this refers to all that is non-real, i.e., the three states of empirical experience. Second is that which is to be known or realized (*jñeya*). Śaṅkara comments that this refers to the knowledge of relationless, non-dual, Ultimate Reality. Third is that which is to be attained or appropriated (*āpya*). This, says Śaṅkara, is the discipline of practical *sādhana*, the accessories of spiritual realization. Fourth is that which is to be made ineffective (*pākyāni*). These are the blemishes or impurities which Śaṅkara calls *kaṣāya* (the passions), such as attraction, repulsion, delusion etc. What

1. *MK* IV. 82.

is to be rejected and what is to be realized comprises the theoretical aspect of the *sādhanā* while what methods are to be utilized and what is to be thus rendered ineffective is the practical side of the *sādhanā*. All this can also be seen another way. On the negative side, Gauḍapāda indicates what is to be rejected and what is to be made ineffective. On the positive side he states what is to be realized and the ways or means to be utilized for that attainment.

While this discipline as a way of life cannot actually be precisely categorized, the tradition does sketch a basic schematization to aid understanding and practice. This can also be seen within Gauḍapāda's practical *sādhanā*. It is the path conceptualized as the three-fold process of *śravaṇa* (listening), *manana* (reflecting) and *nididhyāsana* (contemplating). This three-fold process is given originally in the *Bṛhadāraṇyaka Upaniṣad*, from which Gauḍapāda draws much of his scriptural and philosophical support.

> *Ātman*, verily.. is to be seen by listening to teachings about him, by thinking over his nature, and by contemplation.[1]

This is reflected especially in *MK* II. 35 and 36. In addition to this reference, Gauḍapāda's extensive use of scripture, reasoning and meditational practices attest to this framework.

Gauḍapāda uses a scriptural basis for his teachings. He places *śruti* (revealed scripture) as the highest *pramāṇa*, and frequently alludes to passages as well as gives quotations from texts to support his views and to show the aspirant the nature of reality.[2] *Śravaṇa* as the study of sacred revelation is one of these three-fold means to spiritual attainment. The listening to and study of scripture turns the seeker inwards and directs him to orient his mind towards the self which is sought. It also provides the framework by means of which the aspirant's subsequent experience may be understood and interpreted. Gauḍapāda repeatedly emphasizes the fact that the upaniṣadic truths are not mere utopian dreams but experiences which can be actualized within the life of every practitioner.[3]

1. *Bṛhadāraṇyaka Upaniṣad* II. 4. 5. Compare *Ch. Up.* VI. 14.2 and VIII.7.1.
2. See Chapter III section 2 and especially footnotes on pp. 25 and 26 for specific details.
3. *MK* I.16 for example.

Manana as reflective thinking is the second aspect or stage of this three-fold process. The seeker is asked to reflect and consider the philosophical principles of Advaita and internalize these as a part of his own living faith. He is to see for himself the rightness or validity of these principles. He is to explore the dimensions of his experiences and pursue the practical philosophical enquiry into the nature of the Self. On the one hand, this implies a rational justification of the philosophical principles whereby questions concerning these are reasoned out. This allows the individual to seek out the reasonableness and accuracy of the propositions and also to remove any doubts which he may have about them. This reflection is the method by which doubts and ambiguities about the Vedāntic teachings are removed or at least allayed. On the other hand, this process also becomes *vicāra* or Self-enquiry as a method of reasoning which as it is related to the individual's daily life situation, becomes in itself a type of meditation. Uses of these types of reasoning in the *Māṇḍūkya Kārikā* have been indicated in chapter III above. This process of *manana* or reflection prepares the *sādhaka* for the next stage of *sādhanā* which is *nididhyāsana* or contemplation per se.

The third inter-related aspect of this process, then, is meditation or contemplation. This is the spiritual discipline by means of which the aspirant concentrates his mind on the subtle principle, the Self (*ātman*). It is through this process of concentrated contemplation that the actual experiential attainment of *mokṣa*, or Self-knowledge or wisdom takes place. This is the practice of constant meditation which Gauḍapāda refers to when talking about the practice of *Asparśa-Yoga*. It is the intricacies of this practice and process which he focuses upon at the end of the third *prakaraṇa* of his *Kārikā*.

Śravaṇa and *manana* are incorporated in the *Māṇḍūkya Kārikā* but their direct utilization is not as clearly and directly indicated as is this third aspect of *nididhyāsana*. Yet these three are still very much inter-related herein. They are usually said to be stages or steps of practice and are so at the beginning of the pursuit. When the *sādhaka* is practising his consistent and prolonged *sādhanā*, the three are found to be inter-twined and there is really no succession from one to the other. They are turned to constantly and each supplements the development and success of the other. The three aspects are said to equally contribute to the dawning of knowledge (*jñāna* or *anubhava*) which is the realization of the Self.

3. The Bahiraṅga or Outer Work of Sādhanā

> The mendicant should have no appreciation or greetings (for others), and he should be free from rituals. He should have the body and soul as his support, and he should be dependent on circumstances.
>
> —*MK* II. 37

There are two arbitrary divisions of *sādhanā*. They are the *bahiraṅga*, the outer limb, and the *antaraṅga*, the inner work. The exoteric aspect, *bahiraṅga*, is the preparatory portion of the spiritual pursuit, while the esoteric aspect, the *antaraṅga*, is the real inner work towards the manifestation or actualization of the *anubhava* or direct experience of truth. These two are also actually inseparable and merge constantly in the dynamic process of practising spiritual disciplines. Both are necessary even though the emphasis may be placed on the latter aspects of meditation.

For example, *Patañjali's aṣṭāṅga-yoga* (eight limbs or stages of *yoga* practice) combines both the outer and inner work respectively under the categories of *yama* (restrictions), *niyama* (obligations), *āsana* (posture), *prāṇāyāma* (breath or energy control), *pratyāhāra* (withdrawal of the senses), and then the *saṃyama* which consists of *dhārana* (concentration), *dhyāna* (meditation) and *samādhi* (absorption). The first four correspond to the outer work, the preparatory or preliminary disciplines, while the final four categories relate to the real inner work or meditation. Though given schematically and to a degree successively these of necessity are to be done congruently.

When Gauḍapāda's *Asparśa-Yoga* is interpreted schematically it also reveals such a complete science of the spiritual life. He has not so conveniently organized the system. In the *Māṇḍūkya Kārikā* he goes rather directly to the inner work and to a large extent assumes the contextual situation of the student regarding the knowledge and practice of the outer work (*bahiraṅga*). This then must be culled from the text as a whole.

The major pre-requisite for undertaking the quest for the Self and the consequent practice of *sādhanā* is *mumukṣutva*, the desire for liberation. Feeling the effects of *saṃsāra* the individual must himself strongly desire both release from these circumstances and the goal of freedom, peace and happiness which is consequent with *mokṣa*. It is this very yearning which pushes the aspirant into the spiritual quest that underlies Gauḍapāda's *Kārikā* as a *mokṣa*-or *upadeśa-śāstra* (practical teaching manual). It is this desire which also underlies the teacher-student relationship said to be necessary for fruitful *sādhanā*.

The *guru-śiṣya saṃvāda* (teacher-student discussion) is the foundation of *sādhanā*. Gauḍapāda's text can be seen as a somewhat differently organized form of the dialogue and relationship. Traditionally this text itself is used in this intimate situation as are the *śruti* or sacred scriptural texts. The presence and guidance of an enlightened being either physically or through the medium of scripture is considered indispensable. On the one hand, it is the sage or preceptor who teaches the purport of the scriptures. It is through this that the teachings become meaningful. Not only are the abstruse truths explicated, but also they are seen as embodied in the teacher. Through definition of these subtleties by direct comment and exposition and through the use of various descriptive devices such as reasoning, analogy and illustration the import of the teachings is fully explained. In sum, the preceptor's task is to explain the inexplicable, to define the infinite in finite terms and to awaken the aspirant to the truth of his own being. Further, he is to set forth a complete life program of philosophy, ethics and practices whereby the aspirant through his own self-effort can transform the instruction received into direct personal experience.

Gauḍapāda advocates the taking up of the life of *sannyāsa* (complete renunciation).[1] The life of a renunciate or religious mendicant is considered a necessity for those who want to devote themselves exclusively to *sādhanā* and the spiritual quest. The devoting of one's total life to *Brahmavidyā* implies the wholehearted staying of the mind on *Brahman* to the exclusion of

1. See *MK* II. 37 and the general tenor of the text as a whole.

every other activity. And this cannot relate to the worldly *āśramas* (traditional stages of life), for the duties and obligations imposed therein are a constant distraction and obstruction to the spiritual pursuit. *Brahmaniṣṭhatva* (devotion to *Brahman* only) is possible to the individual who has renounced all duties pertaining to the other three stages of life.

While this is the ideal, Gauḍapāda is aware of the difficulties of the spiritual life and the necessity of compromise for different types of seekers and for those who are at different stages of life.[1] Gauḍapāda first makes the basic distinction among people into those who are knowers, wise or mature and those who are ignorant, child-like or immature.[2] Of the latter group there are several divisons. He suggests three basic categories here : inferior, intermediate and superior which correspond to the different types of seekers at different stages of life. The lower group is comprised of those who are "dull" in that they are spiritually deficient and their inner eye has not yet opened. The middling group consists of those people of average attainments who are torn between worldly duties and the spiritual quest. The superior group is comprised of those few individuals who are well integrated, capable of perceiving the truth and ripe for realization. For the benefit of those of the inferior and middling groups Gauḍapāda advocates various *upāsanās* or devotional meditations prescribed by the scriptures and which can be done within the social framework.[3] Ānandagiri's gloss on *MK* III.16 suggests that men of low vision are those who meditate on the *Kārya-Brahman*, viz, *virāj*, and the middlings on *Kāraṇa-Brahman*, *viz*, *Īśvara*. In *MK* III.1, Gauḍapāda says that these people are pitiable (kṛpaṇa) in comparison to those of superior capabilities who can see the eternal and unoriginated *Brahman*. Yet, the difference in competence cannot really be helped as it is of the nature of plurality. As all must reach the goal, only some will take a longer time than others. Those who are practising meditation have entered the path and their defects will not amount to much if they have a

1. *MK* III. 14-16 and IV. 42-43 (both with Śaṅkara's commentary).
2. *MK* III. 8 and IV. 94.
3. See for example, the *upāsanās* in the first *Vallī* of the *Taittirīya Upaniṣad* and those found throughout the *Chāndogya*.

firm resolve and are persistent in their efforts towards spiritual growth.[1]

The *upāsanās* are given to develop spiritual growth towards non-duality. From devotion and ritual the aspirant moves into contemplative technique depending on his readiness. This is the use of *upāya* or skilful means by the scriptures and preceptors. Realizing the different levels, intellectual capabilities, powers of comprehension, and psychic concentration of the seekers, different teachings and practices are given corresponding to the level of intellectual and moral fibre. This provides the individual with the time and ability to grow and develop spiritually. Giving the teaching of *ajāti* (non-origination) to an individual unable to understand it at the beginning of his spiritual opening may be neither helpful nor creative. Only a few individuals are ready for the higher truths. The masses are afraid of the very idea of the non-manifestation of things (*ajātivāda*) as they are totally given over to and enmeshed with the principle of cause and effect relationships. They also prefer to remain within the familiar world of waking perception alone and place their faith in rituals and so forth. Thus the necessity for a graded or developmental process of spiritual growth.[2]

Some specific preliminary disciplines or practices are given for those pursuing *sādhanā*. They are regarded as useful in preparing the individual for the realization of his true nature. First the aspirant is encouraged to develop and maintain attitudes towards his *sādhanā*. Attitudes such as faith, right understanding, sincere effort and whole-hearted application are considered helpful.[3] Ethical disciplines are also given as an aid in perparation for the inner work.[4] While learning the import of

1. *MK* IV. 43.

2. Gauḍapāda's specific technique of *upāsanā* will be given in the next section.

3. *MK* III. 41 for example.

4. "For Advaita, then, which insists on the sole reality of a distinctionless Oneness, there cannot be any absolute moral laws, principles, or duties. Morality, if it has any enduring spiritual meaning, is simply a quality of the man who realizes his self as "not-different" from *Brahman*. . . .The most basic criterion for moral judgment recommended by Advaita is that those acts, desires, and thoughts that lead the moral agent to the highest good,

the *Vedas* and reflecting upon their teachings, the aspirant is encouraged to also begin getting rid of the defects that obstruct his realization. To cleanse himself of the passions, desire, egoity, and to control the mind, the aspirant is encouraged to develop and practise *viveka* (discrimination), *vairāgya* (dispassion), *abhyāsa* (fixing the mind), and *vicāra* (self-enquiry).[1]

Viveka, which Gauḍapāda here calls *prajñā*, means the discrimination of the real from the unreal. It is the attempt to incorporate the new knowledge and understanding into one's daily life. Actions and choices are based on this new criteria. Only that which is conducive to liberation is to be pursued. Only that which is real is to be valued. Anything else is to be ignored or totally renounced. For all but the non-dual reality is laden with misery. All efforts are to be based on this premise.

The desire for liberation coupled with *viveka* leads the aspirant towards the real. He fixes his thoughts or steadies his mind on one point, which in this case is Ultimate Reality. This is the practice of *abhyāsa*, concentration or continuously thinking of non-dual reality.[2] Realization is said to come easily to the individual who is steadfast in his quest of the Self and in whose mind the thought of *Brahman* always abides.

Knowing the difference between the real and the unreal and concentrating on the real, the aspirant renounces the unreal. This is traditionally called *vairāgya*.[3] *Vairāgya* as detachment and dispassion is regarded as the *conditio sine qua non* of Vedāntic enlightenment. It is one of the important means by which the individual can attain liberation.[4] From conscious dispassion, desirelessness or indifference emerges as the natural outcome of the

---

namely, self-realization, are "good" and that those that lead him towards the fulfilment of egoistic desire, so far as they prevent self-realization, are "bad". . . all activities are. . . transformed and re-directed. . . along the path of realization." Deutsch, *op. cit.*, pp. 100-101.

1. These are not named as such nor is there direct reference to them, although their presence is indicated in the practical instructions. *MK* IV. 79 80 are examples here. The use of the above technical terms became standardized later in the tradition.

2. *MK* II. 36 and III. 43.

3. *MK* III. 43. For a comparison and illustration from the later tradition see Śaṅkara's *Vivekacūḍāmaṇi*, especially verses 373-9.

4. *MK* IV. 79 and 80. The synonymous term *asaṅga* is used here.

realization of the finitude and worthlessness of desires and their objects when contrasted to the infinitude of peace and bliss of the higher experience of the Self. In this way the aspirant becomes unattached (*asaṅga*) to the objects of sense and mentally detached and indifferent to the play of the mind and ego. True and complete detachment is said to be the highest *samādhi*, the condition of liberation wherein the individual is truly *asparśa*, unattached to the play of the world and the world unrelated or never touching the non-dual Self. Thus *vairāgya* means the ever developing trait of dispassion starting with the world of sense-objects and ego-enjoyments and culminating in the state of liberation. Again, here is an example of the goal being the means or method to extract oneself from delusion and pain.

Desire is the root of attachment. Because of this Gauḍapāda says that the individual must become free from desire and its consequences. Unless attachment, fear and anger (*rāga-bhaya-krodha*) are removed no progress is possible.[1] These represent or symbolize the totality of man's deluded state and his consequent bondage with its frustrations, anxieties, sufferings and misery.

The root of desire is the ego (*ahaṅkāra*) which gives the individual a feeling of separateness, independence or autonomy. The cause of man's problems is this false understanding and identification of the ego with the higher Self. The individual, according to Advaita, must decentralize his egoity and realize the illusion of separateness. Liberation is the loss of this false individuality and finitude for the realization of one's own infinitude as the expanse of *Brahman*. The aim of the practices of *sādhanā* is to bring about this purification and prevent this error from re-occurring.[2] This can only be achieved properly if the

1. *MK* II. 35. Compare *Gītā* II. 62-63, III. 37 and IV. 10 ("Completely rid of passion, fear and anger, wholly absorbed in Me, depending on Me, and purified by the penance of wisdom, many have become one with Me even in the past.").

2. "There can be no irreversible peace until the ego, or I-thought, is seen for what it is, namely, a mere notion, a bad habit, and the object of consciousness." John Levy, *The Nature of Man According to the Vedānta*, (London : Routledge and Kegan Paul Ltd., 1956), p. 99.

old habits of the mind are destroyed. Mind and egoism are synonymous. So long as there is the mind, the internal faculty, there will be the individual. Individuality lasts only as long as the mind or ego exists. All of practical *sādhanā* attempts to "destroy" the mind, "annihilate" the ego, "purify" the intellect and "realize" the pure Self.[1]

4. Vicāra and Upāsanā

> One should know *Om*, quarter by quarter; (for) there is no doubt that the quarters (of the Self) are the letters (of *Om*). Having known *Om*, quarter by quarter, one should not think of anything whatsoever.
>
> -*MK* I.24

The first *prakaraṇa* of Gauḍapāda's *Māṇḍūkya Kārikā* includes and is based on the *Māṇḍūkyopaniṣad*. This scriptural text like the *Upaniṣads* as a whole teaches two basic methods or approaches to Self-realization. They are the analytic method of *vicāra* and the contemplative or Yogic method of *upāsanā*. The yogic method of *upāsanā* or devotional meditation uses particular centers or symbols through which the Self may be realized. The analytic method of *vicāra* tries to grasp the Self more directly and concentrates on an enquiry of the Self within the states of experience. The upaniṣad itself appears to advocate a combination of both methods and suggests that they are supplementary rather than opposed techniques. The method of analysis appears to be predominant when the upaniṣad is taken alone. Gauḍapāda's commentary and additions appear to alter and almost reverse this emphasis. For while advocating the analysis of experience and the process of Self-enquiry, he appears to dwell

1. "Mind transcended is ego annihilated. It is for the egocenter that we have the world of ignorance experienced in terms of birth and death, joys and sorrows, successes and failures, etc. Once the ego has been ended there can be no more reincarnations for the *jīva*. The very purpose of this endless pilgrimage through repeated incarnations is but to discover ourselves. Once the hidden Self has been discovered there is no more of this hide and seek play. When I have discovered myself to be nothing other than Self, no more can I, the Self, have the destinies of rebirth or death." Swāmi Chinmayānanda, *op. cit.*, p. 379.

on the use of the *upāsanā* on the *Praṇava, OM.*[1] Further, he places the highest valuation on the contemplation of the *mātrā*-less *OM* as the formless *Brahman* or *Turīya* which he calls the method of *Asparśa Yoga*. Though one appears to be predominant over the other in this way it will become increasingly clear that these two practices are interwoven at all levels of the *sādhanā*.

Vicāra literally means cogitation, the exercise of reason, reflection, deliberation and examination. It is called Self-analysis or enquiry, for the chief function of a knower (*jñāni*) is to know himself. It is the attempt to analyze experience and enquire after the Self therein. It is a kind of dynamic meditation, a method whereby the mind does the work necessary to prepare itself for the deeper meditation on the Self. The movement of Vedāntic *sādhanā* is always one of simplification, of going from what is complex to what is more subtle and simple. In short it is the process of involution or introversion. The *sādhaka* proceeds by way of an analytic search for the existential core, penetrating deeper and deeper by casting off, one by one, the outer wrappings that hide the reality of the Self. Thus the three *avasthās* (states of experience) are examined to discern and sift the imperishable from the perishable, the real from the non-real, the Self from the non-Self and then to directly experience this experiential situation. This is also the process used in the analysis of the five *kośas* or sheaths of man. The method appears to be essentially a method of negation but one which leads to an ultimate affirmation at the end of the quest.[2]

The philosophy or reasoned argumentation of Gauḍapāda's *Māṇḍūkya kārikā* is an aid to this particular practice of *vicāra*. Both use rational thinking when reflecting on experience. The path or way for re-discovering the Self is said to be through

1. MK I. 19-23 suggests this orientation. Also see *MK* I. 24-29.

2. Using the meditation on the *pañca-kośas* the process would follow something like this : "By the mind examine the nature of the five sheaths, by experience determine them, then discard each of them step by step saying 'this is not the Self—this is not the Self,' and by the mind thus grown subtle look for the Self and realize It as the witnessing Consciousness lying beyond the five sheaths."

this very process of right understanding. Gauḍapāda's use of the methods of reason in the *Kārikā* has been indicated previously.[1]

The other major method in the *Māṇḍūkyopaniṣad* and elaborated on in the *Māṇḍūkya Kārikā* is the use of *Upāsanā* (meditation). Śaṅkara has defined the Vedāntic meaning of this term. *Upāsanā* is "the continuous course of thought, not disturbed by any other dissimilar thoughts, toward a particular object supported by scripture."[2] The *ālambana* or support is the object which is the focal point of meditation. The *ālambana* of the Upaniṣadic meditations is *Brahman*. There are numerous *upāsanās* detailed throughout the early upaniṣads. But the best *ālambana* for the *upāsanā* on *Brahman* is said to be the sacred syllable *OM*. This particular technique is given the central and unique position in the *Māṇḍūkyopaniṣad*.[3]

There are two kinds of *upāsanā* which can be seen combined in this particular *upāsanā* on *Oṅkāra*, as given in the texts at hand. *Pratikopāsanā* is the kind which is symbolical or concerned with external symbols (*pratika*). These are the forms of devotional meditations or worship wherein the object is taken as the representative symbol of God or the Absolute. Rather than being identical with the Absolute, this reality is sought to be realized "through" the *pratika* and not "as" the *pratika*. This is evident in the idea that the *sādhaka* is to take the *pratika* as God rather than taking God as the *pratika*, for God is infinitely superior to the *pratika*. The other kind is called *ahaṅgrahopāsanā* which involves the contemplation of the Self. This is an inner (*āntara*) form of meditation wherein there is an identification of the object contemplated with the subject himself. Here the

1. See Chapter III section 3 in particular and the process of *manana* in section 2 of this chapter. Chapter V section 1 is also pertinent here. It is also quite possible that Gauḍapāda used the process of dialectical reasoning as a method for this pursuit of Self-realization. For there is a definite link between dialectical reasoning and intuitive realization. This is the use of philosophy as a contemplative technique, although one of rigorous negation.

2. Śaṅkara's introduction to *Ch. Up.* I. 1. 1. See also his commentary on *PUp.* 5, *BS.* I. 1. 11, and IV. 1. 7.

3. See *Kaṭha* I. 2. 15-17; *Praśna* V. 2-7; *Muṇḍaka* II. 2. 4; *Taittirīya* I. 8; *Maitrī* VI. 2-5, 14, 22, 24, 25; *Chāndogya* I. 1. 1, I. 1. 5, 6, I. 1. 8, I. 4. 4, I. 5. 1, II. 13. 2, II. 13. 3, VI. 2, *Māṇḍūkya* 1-12.

Self is supposed to be not merely a symbol or manifestation but the very Absolute itself. There are two classes of this kind, *saguṇa* and *nirguṇa*. When some qualities are attributed to the Self and the meditation is upon them, the *upāsanā* is called *saguṇa*. It is termed a *nirguṇa* form when all qualities and attributes are stripped off the Self and the *upāsanā* seeks for an identification with the very essence of Being.

The *Māṇḍūkyopaniṣad* is solely concerned with the meditation on the *praṇava*, *OM*. The first verse begins with the phrase, "the syllable *OM* is all this," and then this is elaborated upon in fuller detail in the subsequent verses. The *Āgamaprakaraṇa* of Gauḍapāda's *Kārikā* is the fuller exposition of these terse verses. First, he dedicates this chapter to the explanation of the scope and significance of *OM* as theory. Secondly, the *upāsanā* on *Oṅkāra* is offered as a practical meditation technique. This is indicative of his teaching trend whereby he begins with the enunciation of the religious and philosophical presuppositions of the system as background, rationalization and preparation for the meditative practice.

It is clear from the last verse of the first *prakaraṇa* that Gauḍapāda intends to advocate this *upāsanā* as the basis of his meditative discipline.[1] *Kārikās* I. 24-29 extol the *upāsanā* and the *upāsaka* (the practiser of the technique) as a whole and especially its *amātra* or *mātrā*-less aspect. In *MK* I. 24 Gauḍapāda gives his definitive statement on technique.

> One should know *OM*, quarter by quarter : (for) there is no doubt that the quarters (of the Self) are the letters (of *OM*). Having known *OM*, quarter by quarter, one should not think of anything whatsoever.

This suggests a progressive discipline of meditation upon the various parts of the *mantra* working from the grossest to the subtlest levels of experience. The *upāsanā* is an all-inclusive and synthetic technique which incorporates many individual methods and brings them together on a graded or evolutionary scale leading the aspirant towards deeper spiritual experience. There

---

1. *MK* I. 29.

is no necessity of meditating upon anything else. Spiritual development or unfolding will ensue through the persistent utilization of this discipline.

The syllable *OM* (*AUM*) is the symbol indicative of the *Brahman-Ātman* idea. *OM* as a sound principle is said to be inclusive of all sounds and hence is called the support of the world of speech (*vāk-prapañca*).[1] The support or ground of the world is *Brahman*. On the basis of this homology the sound *OM* is made to stand for the *Ātman* or *Brahman*. Through its use, the *upāsaka* is said to attain *Brahma-vidyā*.

The *praṇava-yoga* given here is based on the principle of identification or equation (*sāmānyadharma*). *MK* I. 19-22 suggests the process happening in each meditation. Gauḍapāda calls this *mātrāsampratipatti*, knowing the *mātrās* to be identical with the *pādas*[2] and *oṅkārasya pādaśovidyā*, the knowledge of the *mātrās* of *OM* as the *pādas* of the Self.[3] Thus the letter "*a*" corresponds to *Viśva* who represents the gross universe, the waking state.[4] The letter "*u*" corresponds to *Taijasa* who represents the dream state.[5] The letter "*m*" corresponds to *Prājña* who represents the deep sleep state of experience.[6] The last identification is that of the *amātra* or *mātrā*-less aspect of *AUM* with the state of *Turiya* which conceptually represents the non-dual Self or Pure Consciousness.[7]

The *Māṇḍūkyopaniṣad* and Gauḍapāda's *Kārikā* give reasons for these identifications which are intended to further enable the

1. It is said that any experience in the universe, anything that is seen or felt, can be communicated through phonetic sounds. Sanskrit is a phonetic system which incorporates the various possible utterances which man is capable of making. Further, the syllable *OM* (*AUM*) is said in itself to represent the entire range of verbal sounds. "A" has its origin in the throat, "U" from the middle of the mouth and "M" is produced by the lips. Without these three sounds, no word can be produced or pronounced. The letters represent the beginning, middle and end of all phonetic sounds. All sounds can be thus contained within the range of these three sounds.

2. *MK* I. 19.

3. *MK* I. 24.

4. *MUp* 9, *MK* I. 19.

5. *MUp* 10, *MK* I. 20.

6. *MUp* 11, *MK* I. 21.

7. *MUp* 8.

sādhaka to concentrate on the significance of *OM*. The letter "*a*" and the waking state represented by *Viśva* are regarded as identical because of the common quality of being first (*ādi*) as well as that of pervading (*āpti*). As "*a*" is the first sound-component of *OM*, so is *Viśva* the first aspect of the Self. And as the vowel-sound "*a*" is said to be pervasive of all speech, *Viśva* is pervasive of the universe. The second *mātrā* "*u*" and the second *pāda Taijasa* share the common qualities of exaltation (*utkarṣa*) and intermediacy (*ubhayatva*). The excellence of "*u*" is due to its following "*a*", while similarly *Taijasa* exceeds *Viśva* because of its superior positioning. And as "*u*" is intermediate between "*a*" and "*m*", so also is *Taijasa* between *Viśva* and *Prājña*. The common features identifying "*m*" and *Prājña* are said to be measure (*miti* or *māna*) and absorption (*apiti* or *laya*). The *mātrā* "*m*" is the measure of the others as upon the repeated chanting of *OM*, the "*a*" and "*u*", as it were, merge and emerge from "*m*". *Prājña* is the measure of *Viśva* and *Taijasa* as these evolve from it at creation and return to it at dissolution. This can be seen again in that the worlds of waking and dream disappear in deep sleep and from that very sleep they emerge again. This shows both the measuring (*māna*) and the disappearing (*laya*) aspects of this identification. With the exception of the second feature of *Prājña*, each letter stands for the first letter of the words signifying features of the Self in its manifestations as *Viśva*, *Taijasa* and *Prājña*. Thus "*a*" stands for *ādi* and *āpti*, "*u*" for *utkarṣa* and *ubhayatva*, and "*m*" for *miti* or *māna*. From this it is clear that the *mātrās* are used in these meditations as mnemonics.

The fourth *mātrā* is said to be represented by the point (*bindu*) of the *anusvāra* over the "*m*". But this is really *amātra* or moraeless. It is the silence into which the sound *OM* culminates. It is the partless or distinctionless *OM*. As such it is identical with the Self designated here as *Turīya* or Pure Consciousness which transcends the distinctions inherent in the forms of the Self known as *Viśva*, *Taijasa* and *Prājña*.[1]

1. *MUp* 12.

Māṇḍūkyopaniṣad 9-12 eulogizes this practice of meditation by specifying the results of each stage. He who knows *Vaiśvānara* (i.e., *Viśva*) thus obtains all desires and becomes the foremost among people, i.e., prominent, well-respected, adored and revered. This suggests someone who has achieved a higher level of self-development than the ordinary man and who has the ability to deal with the empirical world in a balanced or harmonious fashion. He who knows *Taijasa* in this way exalts or increases the current of knowledge and becomes equal to all. This suggests the development of the mind and intellect to the point of possessing superior knowledge and also the ability to relate to others, as well as them to oneself, on an egalitarian level. Also, there is said to be none born in his line who is not a knower of *Brahman.* He who knows the identity of *Prājña* and "*m*" measures the whole world, that is to say, he knows its reality, and he becomes the place of absorption in that he becomes the Self in its causal state.[1] Finally, he who truly knows the partless *OM* as *Turīya* realizes the Self and retains this thenceforth.

These benefits or results suggest the fulfilment of the "well-developed" personality characteristic of each state of consciousness. For the results are different in accordance with the emphasis laid on its constituents. The fruits of the meditations of the first three appear to be rather mundane gains in comparison to the result of liberation or the realization of the Self which is said to accrue from the *upāsanā* on the *amātra* aspect of *OM*. Other upaniṣads list the benefits or results of this type of meditation on *Oṅkāra* but there are some fundamental differences.[2] The emphasis appears to be placed more on the actual practice of the meditation exercises rather than on the gaining of the fruits thereof which seem only to be the enticements to motivate practice.

1. Additional interpretation from Śaṅkara's commentary on *MUp* 11.

2. For similar results of meditation on the *mātrās* of *OM* in the other *Upaniṣads* see Mahadevan, *op. cit.*, p. 177-178. "The implication of the eulogy is that the *sādhaka* should understand the significance of *OM* and meditate on it; the deeper the comprehension, the greater will be the benefit."

In *MK* I. 2, Gauḍapāda gives some additional details which are possibly relevant here. He assigns localities in the body for the different expressions of consciousness for the purpose of meditation. *Viśva* is said to reside in the right eye (*dakṣiṇa-akṣi*). This is both symbolic and realistic as it suggests experience and perception through the senses beginning with sight.[1] *Taijasa* is to be meditated on in the mind (*manas*) which again suggests a symbolic and a realistic attribution of subjective experiencing. *Prājña* has its seat in the ether of the heart (*ākāśa*). The heart-space is symbolic of the center or core of man's inmost Self and suggests that at the time of the absorption of consciousness in deep sleep one returns to oneself. One of the fundamental purposes of this locating of the three selves is to indicate that all of them are located within the individual. Further, these are to be found within the waking state itself and as such this teaches their fundamental unity. Thus, the one Self can be found as three in one body while ultimately remaining unique in its non-dual nature.[2] Most important here is that the practice remains experiential in that the place of practice is within the microcosm of the meditator.

In the final verses of the *Āgamaprakaraṇa* following the last verse of the *Māṇḍūkyopaniṣad*, Gauḍapāda stresses the real value of the meditation on *Oṅkāra*. In *MK* I. 23 he again points out that "*a*" leads to *Viśva*, "*u*" to *Taijasa*, "*m*" to *Prājña*, and that there is no "attainment" of anything in the *amātra*. Ānandagiri adds that this means the respective attainment or full realization of the gross universe or waking state, the subtle universe or dream state, the causal condition or deep sleep successively. Further, he explains that the purpose of meditation is to lead the *sādhaka* from the grosser states to the subtler successively until he reaches the condition wherein all duality is removed. This is the *Turiya* or non-dual Self wherein there is no distinction of attainer, object-to-be-attained, and the attainment itself. The achievement of the last stage of practice is the ultimate goal of the earlier stages as well. It is the final

1. This is affirmed by Śaṅkara's commentary on *MK* I. 2.
2. *MK* I. 1 and Śaṅkara's commentary.

movement of the *ahaṅgraha upāsanā*, the turning inward towards one's own Self. Thus the emphasis or real import of the technique is upon this latter aspect, the *mātrā*-less aspect of the *upāsanā* on *Oṅkāra*.

This is the unique Vedāntic *sādhanā*. It is the movement from concentration on a *pratika*, to higher forms of *upāsanā*, culminating in Advaitic contemplation traditionally called *Nididhyāsana*. *Oṅkāra* as the symbol of *Brahman* can be utilized in many ways, but the highest method is the movement into *Jñāna Sādhanā*. Through understanding the higher meaning and import of *OM* and merging the repetition of the three syllables into the *amātra* aspect, the *upāsaka* lets the three states of consciousness merge and dissolve in that profound passive silence of *Turiya* and simply remaining in that, lets the *Ātman* unfold there.

The process theoretically proceeds as follows. The meditation begins by taking the *ālambana* and using it as the point of attention for concentration. It is useful in steadying the mind-modifications and making the thought-current flow in one direction. The practice of *upāsanā* is the directing of a continuous flow of thought towards the object of meditation without any contrary mental intervention. Itssuccess is traditionally likened to the steady stream of the flow of oil being poured. In this way the centrifugal tendency of the mind is eventually arrested and becomes one-pointed like the flame of a lamp in a windless place. The process of the technique here is to economize the production of thought and to control and regulate the flow of thinking in the mind. The mind becomes one-pointed by continuous chanting and concentration. When the mind is unified with the sound *OM* there is no particularized thought of a discursive nature and it becomes identified with or absorbed into the sound syllable. The mind's *vṛttis* or thought-currents are silenced in the *Brahma-vṛtti*. This is accomplished by the continuous chanting of *OM* in the mind wherein the meditator observing the rising, falling and dying away of the sound-syllable finally merges into and experiences the ensuing silence. Upon reaching the silence, the *upāsaka* does not try to initiate new thought waves, but tries only to delve into that silence and to abide therein. This is *śama* or stillness of the mind which is called the state of "no-mind" (*amanibhāva*). This is the *Turiya* or *Brahman* experienced as Pure Consciousness. Thus, through the progressive movement from the use of the lower *upāsanās* the seeker practises the higher meditation which Gauḍapāda advocates and designates as *Asparśa Yoga*.

It should be noted that this is a new departure from earlier upaniṣads as well as from other teachings and techniques. The other older upaniṣads which describe the practice deal with *Oṅkāra* in its three-fold aspect and without either the awareness or at least the emphasis on the *Turiya* aspect. In this respect, both the *Māṇḍūkyopaniṣad* and Gauḍapāda's *Kārikā* mark a new or unique historical phase in the development of the teaching as well as in the technique for its experiential realization.[1]

Gauḍapāda concludes his exposition of the *praṇavadhyāna* by praising it and those who practise it. The mind should be concentrated on the *praṇava*; one should not think of anything else whatsoever.[2] *Praṇava* is the *Brahman* beyond fear, and for a man ever fixed in *Brahman* there can be no fear anywhere.[3] *Praṇava* is the lower *Brahman* (*Īśvara*) and also the higher *Brahman*.[4] It is the beginning, middle and end of everything.[5] Yet it is without cause and without effect.[6] There is nothing besides it, nothing outside it, nor anything that follows it. *Praṇava* is known, on the one hand, as the Lord seated in the hearts of all,[7] and on the other, as the auspicious entity, without measures and possessed of infinite dimension, where all duality ceases.[8] Thus the *sādhaka* who knows the *Praṇava* in this way is said to attain identity with *Turiya* or *Brahman* immediately.[9] He is indeed the real sage, the truly enlightened or Self-realized man.

---

1. Gauḍapāda himself appears to be aware of its uniqueness in *MK* III. 39. This will be discussed further in the next section.
2. *MK* I. 24.
3. *MK* I. 25.
4. *MK* I. 26.
5. *MK* I. 27.
6. *MK* I. 26.
7. *MK* I. 28.
8. *MK* I. 29.
9. *MK* I. 27.

To further emphasize the *Turiya* aspect of the *Oṅkāra upāsanā*, in chapter three of the *Māṇḍūkya Kārikā* Gauḍapāda criticizes those *upāsakas* who are practising the inferior forms of meditation. While not denying the efficacy of the stages of this *upāsanā* from the empirical point of view for mediocre aspirants, Gauḍapāda[1] firmly promotes the *nididhyāsana* technique based upon the ideal of the *aja Brahman* as ultimately the highest and only reality. From this perspective, he calls the ordinary *upāsaka* "pitiable" or "narrow-minded" (*kṛpaṇa*) since he who practises the inferior forms of meditation stays in the conditioned *Brahman*.[2] He directs criticism towards their short-sightedness, their limited understanding or belief, and suggests that they are still involved in binding conceptual structures superimposed upon reality. This conceptualization and all that follows from it necessarily influences their understanding and practice of meditation.[3] Gauḍapāda's *Kārikā* is thus seen to be a text primarily directed to the highest students of the spiritual path, while the other and lower philosophies and techniques are prescribed out of compassion and the recognition of the gradual spiritual development of the *sādhaka*. For the highest aspirants, Gauḍapāda prescribes the *Turiya upāsanā* which he later calls the practice of *Asparśa Yoga*.[4] This and only this method leads to *ātmasatyānubodha*, the

1. *MK* III. 16.
2. *MK* III. 1.
3. On the one hand, Gauḍapāda allows a place for *bhakti* or devotion to God (*Īśvara*) in his *sādhanā* as *AUM* is the Lord, ever present in the minds and hearts of men as the *antaryāmin* (*MK* I. 28). While on the other hand, he is very critical of all positions other than that from the *paramārtha* perspective. "There is an inherent logical contrarinesss in a philosophy that permits a devotional approach to a Lord who has a relation with the devotee as part and whole, when to the same devotee the Lord Himself has manifested as the pluralistic world. If the Supreme Reality has manifested Himself as the pluralistic world of phenomena, then the devotee himself is, in fact, nothing but the same Reality. After accepting this theory of creation, for any devotee to worship the Lord who is considered to be something other than himself would, naturally, be a palpable contradiction which has serious implications leading to imperfect thinking. It is this idea that has been condemned by this opening stanza of this chapter." Swāmī Chinmayānanda, *op. cit.*, p. 198. See also Śaṅkara's commentary on *MK* III. 1 and 2.
4. *MK* III. 39.

direct experiential realization of the highest truth which is the Self.

5. Asparśa Yoga

> I bow down to that *yoga* known as *asparśa* which is joyful to all beings, beneficial, free from dispute, non-contradictory, and set forth in the scriptures. —*MK* IV. 2

Asparśa Yoga is the key soteriological term in the *Māṇḍūkya Kārikā*. Mentioned twice at prominent places, *MK* III. 39 and IV. 2, this term embodies the quintessence of Gauḍapāda's liberation philosophy and practice. In the third book, the *Advaita prakaraṇa*, the reference comes after he has shown the various dualist positions to be faulty and that the truth of Advaita is to be accepted and then realized. It is in the *upadeśa* (teaching) section of this chapter during a discussion of meditation techinque and theory that Gauḍapāda states the Advaita conceptualization of practice as being called *Asparśa Yoga.*[1] Further, Gauḍapāda opens the fourth *prakaraṇa* with two obeisances or saluations, the first to his teacher and the second one immediately following is to this *yoga*. Thus *Asparśa Yoga* is given the highest place in Gauḍapāda's text and in his soteriological system.

The above salutation is eulogistic on the one hand and also points to concrete realizations on the other. He states that this *yoga* promotes the happiness of all its practitioners and is conducive to the well-being of all. Further, he suggests that it is free from dispute and contradiction both philosophically and experientially. Finally, he suggests that this conceptualization of philosophy and practice is well known. This is reiterated again in *MK* III. 39 with more clarity but still with no scriptural references. Śaṅkara (circa 788-820 A.D.) declares it as having been instructed in the scriptures, i.e., the *Upaniṣads*.

The term itself is not to be found in the *Upaniṣads* nor the *Gitā* and it is quite conceivable that Gauḍapāda coined the designation to express the Advaita conceptualization of soteriological theory and practice. Śaṅkara in his commentary

1. These verses are given in full in Appendix I.

on *MK* IV. 2 refers to this concept as "*advaita darśana yoga*," the practical teaching of the holders of the non-dualist perspective. Further he comments,

> *Asparśa Yoga* is that *yoga*, which has no *sparśa*, touch, relationship, with anything at any time; it is of the very nature of *Brahman* .To the knowers of *Brahman* . . . it is well known as the *Yoga* free from all relationships.[1]

This term is a compound of the two words *asparśa* and *yoga*. These should be further investigated here. First, the principal term of the compound. The noun *yoga* is found widely used in Sanskrit literature and in the religious and philosophical pórtions thereof in particular. It is a multi-valent term implying several distinct meanings and is also used traditionally in several ways. From the root, *yuj*, meaning "to join," its etymological "meaning is the process of joining together" any two things either objectively or subjectively. A secondary and specialized sense of the term in religious and philosophical literature suggests that it means "a process by which it seeks to restore the Self, Spirit, or Soul to its original state." There are several aspects herein. It either emphasizes a particular means or method recommended or it emphasizes the goal to be reached. From Gauḍapāda's verse and Śaṅkara's commentary both of these emphases can be construed, though the predominant stress appears to be upon it as method or process. This will be further explored after the term *asparśa* is enquired into.

The first member of the compound, *asparśa*, determines the meaning of the compound as a whole by emphasizing its special characteristic or principal feature. *Asparśa* is the simple negation of the term *sparśa* which literally means "touch" or "contact". The classical reference of this term is in the idea of the mind's contact with external objects through the sense-organs. This is one of the denotations of Gauḍapāda's own use of the term *sparśa* in *MK* IV. 41.

The term *asparśa* itself is not found elsewhere but references to the term *sparśa* in yogic contexts are common. The use of this latter term in the *Gītā* is relevant here. In the *Gītā* it is

1. From Śaṅkara's commentary on *MK* IV. 2.

used in the sense given above. In *G* II. 14 the term *mātrā-sparśa* is used indicating that life is an interaction between the senses and the objects of the phenomenal world. Life consists of an ongoing series of the interactions between these two. This is reaffirmed in *G* V. 21 and 22 where the term refers to the contact of the mind with the senses. The context here is that this contact or relationship is the cause of worldly pain and suffering. And in *G* V. 21 the antidote of non-attachment to the external senses (*bāhyasparśeṣvasaktātmā*) is indicated. This process is undertaken during the meditation practice advocated. One of the definitions of *yoga* given in *G* VI. 23 is pertinent here. It is defined as the state of severance from union with pain (*duḥkha-saṃyoga-viyoga*) which is none other than the pain born of the contact (*sparśa*) of the senses with the objects of the manifold universe.

From this definitive background, the development and meaning of the term *Asparśa Yoga* can be easily seen. While *sparśa-yoga* refers to contact with sense-objects being the cause of misery, *asparśa-yoga* suggests that the disconnection or freedom from this source of pain leads to happiness. On a more abstract level this term refers to the concept of contact in the sense of relationship per se. All such relationships consisting of two factors, such as the senses contacting the objects, are found in the realm of relativity in the *vyāvahārika* states of waking, dream and deep sleep. The *pāramārthika* or ultimate truth is that there is no duality, that the Self is the non-dual *Turiya* or *Brahman*. In the nature of *Brahman* there is no *sparśa* of any sort. This is stated clearly by Gauḍapāda in *MK* IV. 26-28 and 72.[1] Thus this term *asparśa* directly refers to the highest reality, the absolute *Brahman*. This is verified by Śaṅkara in his commentary on *MK* IV. 2.

Thus there are two meanings of the term *Asparśa Yoga*. On the philosophical level, the term implies the realization of non-duality, i.e., of *Turiya* or *Brahman*. In this sense it could be called the "Non-dual Yoga" or the "Yoga of the Non-dual." On the level of religious practice, the term refers to the discipline, path,

1. Note the use of the verb *spṛś* here : *cittaṁ na saṃspṛśatyartham* (Consciousness does not come into contact with objects).

method or process whereby the *sādhaka* attains this condition of being one with Ultimate Reality.

Normally, an Advaita Vedāntin will not use the term *yoga* in his discussion for several reasons. Firstly, the strictly non-dualist perspective as stated by Gauḍapāda himself in *MK* II. 32 and III. 36 precludes the very talk of "someone" doing "something" to attain "some goal." In *MK* III. 36, Gauḍapāda states that in regard to the non-dual *Brahman* there can be no ceremony, conduct or practice (*upacāra*). Yet on an empirical level, it is obvious that the tradition does suggest that there are methods by which the realization of one's true nature can be facilitated or at least precipitated.[1] Secondly, the term *yoga* itself denotes the coming into union of two factors, one separated from the other. This is similar to the idea of *sparśa* suggested above. The problem here is that the use of this kind of language is dualist oriented. Even to suggest that the *yoga* indicated here is the union of the individual soul or self (*jīva*) with the Supreme Soul (*Brahman*) alludes to the delusory belief in duality. Nonetheless, the term is used in a uniquely Advaitic sense to refer metaphorically to union with the Self, not in the sense of gaining union with something separate, but rather in the realization of the unity of the Self as being without a second, i.e., as being the subtlest essence as well as the totality of non-dual reality. Further, there are numerous references to *yoga* within advaitic contexts of the upaniṣads as well as in the literature of the developed tradition. The use of the term *yoga* in the sense of spiritual practice or discipline in general appears to be common to all the religio-philosophical traditions in India. Also, Gauḍapāda is teaching from within the milieu of *yoga* practitioners and many of his comments in this particular section are directly aimed at the erroneous views and practices of the various *yoga* disciplines. So it is quite appropriate that he uses the term *yoga* in his discussions.

1. This seeming paradox of stating 'there is no practice to realize enlightenment on the one hand, and on the other, advocating disciplines' will be dealt with further in the next section.

Contextually, the term *Asparśa Yoga* refers to the practice or process by which the aspirant seeks to achieve this soteriological goal. The term is used in *MK* III. 39 which lies halfway within the *upadeśa-śāstra* portion of the *Advaita prakaraṇa* (III. 32-46). This section comes after Gauḍapāda's refutation of the dualist views of reality and the establishment of the Advaita position. He begins the *upadeśa* section after the mention of *māyā* and "mind creation" which sets the stage for a discussion of the nature of the mind and its relation to bondage and liberation (*MK* III. 29-38). This is specifically related to the notion of *amanibhāva*, the state of "non-mind," which is given supreme valuation here by Gauḍapāda. At this point the idea of *Asparśa Yoga* is introduced in *MK* III. 39 and is followed by a discussion of topics related to the actual practice of meditation. Thus it appears that *Asparśa Yoga* refers to the nature of the process of liberation or Self-realization in this specifically Advaita Vedānta context.

Finally, there is the question as to whether this is a new species of *yoga* or one already known but named differently by Gauḍapāda. There are no scriptural references cited in the *Māṇḍūkya Kārikā* in this regard, though he has used the indeclinables *vai nāma* while mentioning the term. From this the inference is that he meant a familiar kind of *yoga*. Śaṅkara corroborates this in his commentary. On *MK* III. 39 he states that *Asparśa Yoga* is well-known in the *Upaniṣads* and on *MK* IV. 2 says that it is well-known by that name to the knowers of *Brahma*. Śaṅkara himself does not cite any scriptural support here either.

The term itself is not actually used in any *śruti* texts. Yet the content of the theory and of the practice is discernible from these sources. There are other such terms used in scriptural literature such as *Adhyātma-yoga* (*Kaṭhopaniṣad* I. 2. 12), *Sannyāsa-yoga* (*Māṇḍūkyopaniṣad* III. 2-6), etc. and various terms in the *Gītā* such as *Dhyāna-yoga*, *Sāṅkhya-yoga* and *Ātmasaṃyama-yoga*. The details of the practices associated with these terms are at times vague but the similarities are clear. Gauḍapāda in his *Kārikā* has brought the details of practice into a consistent whole for explicit teaching purposes. Though being essentially based on upaniṣadic details, the development is Gauḍapāda's own unique contribution.[1]

6. The Nature of Asparśa Yoga

> *Brahman* is birthless, sleepless, dreamless, nameless, formless, ever effulgent, everything, and a knower. (With regard to It) there is not the the least possibility of ceremony.
>
> —*MK* III. 36

Asparśa Yoga is Gauḍapāda's designation for the unique *Advaita* or non-dualist orientation to practices or techniques of liberation. The goal he sets is, in yogic terminology, called *nirvikalpa samādhi* which, he states, is identical with non-dual *Brahman*, the Self (*ātman*), and Pure Consciousness (*citta*). From the Advaita perspective this is called *Brahma-vidyā*, the experiential knowledge of *Brahman*. Gauḍapāda uses both *advaita* and *yoga* terminology and brings forth a new synthesis in his *Kārikā*. Although there is a synthesis of language and practice to some extent, Gauḍapāda is careful to point out the subtle differences between traditional *yoga* forms and the higher practices of the advaitic discipline. In this way his designation of *Asparśa Yoga* is to a large extent a new addition to the previous descriptions in scriptural literature. For Gauḍapāda is concerned with a more precise definition of the nature and the process of the advaita discipline which is set forth in the *Upaniṣads* and explicated further in his own *Kārikā*.

This process is contingent upon understanding the nature of Consciousness, its manifestations, its functioning and the ways or methods by which it can be known. This has been dealt with previously in chapter V. To briefly reiterate, Gauḍapāda uses the terms *manas*, *citta*, and *vijñāna* to signify consciousness. He uses them in two ways but deliberately so as to show their

---

1. The above discussion, following the Advaita Vedānta orientation of the present work, has not dealt with the contention by some scholars concerning the possible Buddhist nature of this *Asparśa Yoga* material. To deal with these hypotheses at this point is superfluous to the argument being presented. For references see Mahadevan, *op. cit.*, and Bhattacharya, *op. cit.*

actual unity or sameness. On the one hand, Consciousness as pure non-dual Being is the essence or substratum of reality. On the other hand, these terms are taken to mean the individual consciousness (*antaḥ-karaṇa*) or the empirical mind (*manas*). So it is within "consciousness" that the *sādhaka* practises. The task appears to be one of sublimating or sublating the manifestations of Consciousness and experiencing pure Consciousness.

Psychologically this process is described as bringing the "mind" under control, allowing the "mind-process" to cease and thus attaining the state of "non-mind." This, then, is a situation wherein what is already present is realized or known and that which covers it is removed. To do this the empirical mind per se must be transcended and that substratum through which it operates must be directly experienced. Thus, as this involves undermining the very structure of the mind, the Vedāntic *nididhyāsana* (meditation and contemplation) cannot be a technique involving the mind and its processes. By its very nature it must be a subtle technique of going behind, as it were, the mind-structure itself.[1] This helps to understand the seeming paradox that there is no practice by which one can realize *Brahman* and yet that there are directions and disciplines given for such a purpose.

All this becomes even clearer when Gauḍapāda discusses the importance of the difference between the state of *suṣupti* and that of the non-dual *Turiya* in reference to the meditation practice. Cause and effect do not exist in *Turiya* whereas *Prājña* is said to be conditioned by cause.[2] Non-perception of duality is common to both but *Prājña* is still within the structure of dualism.[3] *Prājña* is a state of unconsciousness, a state of deep dreamless sleep whereas there is neither dream nor sleep in *Turiya*.[4] As a non-conscious state *Prājña* does not comprehend anything, itself nor others,[5] whereas *Turiya* is the witness of

1. Swāmi Bhoomananda Tirtha, *Brahma Vidya Abhyasa*, II (Trichur : Narayana Ashrama Thapovanam, 1970), p. 82.
2. *MK* I.11.
3. *MK* I.13.
4. *MK* I. 14.
5. *MK* I. 12.

everything.[1] Finally, it is stated that in the *Prājña* state, due to the lack of awareness, there is basic ignorance of reality, whereas in *Turiya* reality is fully realized.[2]

This last point is the crux of the problem. For Gauḍapāda's *Kārikā* as a soteriological treatise is mainly concerned on the practical level of meditative experience with this subtle but vitally important differentiation.[3] Gauḍapāda is particularly concerned with making clear the distinction between the Advaita *samādhi* and the traditional yogic *samādhi*. They are as different from each other as are *Turiya* and deep sleep, to which Gauḍapāda compares them. Both of these conditions are *nir-vikalpa*, i.e., without the modifications of consciousness. Both schools of thought accept *nirvikalpa samādhi* as the acme of spiritual experience. But Gauḍapāda makes the further distinction between levels of experience within this condition as he points out that the mere achievement of this *samādhi*, though pleasant, is not true liberation. There is much more to be done upon the attainment of such experiences and that the quality of such is to be educed.

Gauḍapāda thus talks of three basic states of consciousness from an experiential point of view in difference to the traditional two aspects of *vikalpa* and *nirvikalpa*.[4] The *vikalpa* aspect of consciousness is the empirical consciousness of everyday experience. The *nirvikalpa* aspect is that state bereft of all thought constructions. All schools accept this. But Gauḍapāda calls this second one a condition or state of unconsciousness or lack of consciousness rather than the experience of ever-present pure consciousness which he now posits as the third condition.

This differentiation on a practical level suggests entirely different objectives as well as techniques of practice to attain such goals.[5] The traditional *yoga* methodology of *dhyāna* or

1. *MK* I. 12.
2. *MK* I. 15 and 16.
3. *MK* III. 34-36 and 39-40 in particular.
4. *MK* III. 34-35 and 46.
5. One of the main differences here is the way classical Pātañjala Yoga defines the problem and the goal. The problem here concerns the disequilibrium of the three *guṇas* of *prakṛti* (matter) and the goal of the *kaivalya* (isolation) of *puruṣa* (spirit) from *prakṛti*. The theoretical conceptualization of Advaita, especially Gauḍapāda here in this specific instance, is quite different.

meditation is typified by the *Yoga Sūtra* definition as *citta-vṛtti-nirodhaḥ*, the restraint or suppression of the mind-forms. Rather than this orientation, Gauḍapâda advocates the practice of Advaita *nididhyāsana* which can be termed sublimation or transformation. Instead of mechanically and effortfully restraining the mind-forms, this practice intends to transform the mind into its pristine condition of non-mind with the consequent realization of the Self or Pure Consciousness due to the sublation or loss of the false impositions of the mind-forms upon experience. The mind is under control (*manasaḥ nigṛhitasya*),[1] not in the sense of suppression or restraint (*nirodha*) of the mental activities, but in that the process of imagination (*vikalpa*) ceases and there is no identification with its products or distraction by its agitations, and pure awareness remains without the super-impositions of duality.

It is not going into an unconscious trance-like state (*laya*). Suppression of the mind merely leads to a dull inert experience as in stupor, sleep, or death. In these states the mind is not active and the experience is only remembered after the fact. While in such a state the individual knows nothing, the mind merely lies dormant, and upon resumption of the waking state all of the psychological forces resume their previous functioning. Further, these states are periodic and ephemeral and only maintained through rigorous effort and persistent withdrawal from normal consciousness. Gauḍapāda points out the futility of such methods to attain peace and liberation.

Thus the classical *nirodha* method refers to the deliberate efforts to suppress or restrain the mind by negating its existence, functions and the results which those functions produce. On the other hand, the Advaita method, called *Asparśa Yoga* (*nigṛhita mana*) for distinction here by Gauḍapāda, refers to the control of the mind through its sublimation or transformation. The method of *Asparśa Yoga* can be called the "non-mind technique" for its task is to render the mind quiescent or motion-

It should be noted that the present writer argues differently than Swâmi Nikhilānanda in his notes to the text where he tries to blend the two perspectives. It becomes confusing there as the separation is necessary.

I. *MK* III. 34-35 and 40.

less (*aniṅgana*).[1] Mind in the form of the experience of empirical consciousness is to be transformed into its real nature as pure non-dual consciousness. For the mind should be regarded as something which has no independent existence. Its existence depends upon the world and its objects which are posited as different from it. Mind as such always remains within the sphere of duality, and distracted by the play of the pairs of opposites it does not recognize its essence as the substratum of pure non-dual Consciousness.

The *Asparśa Yoga* "non-mind technique," then, is one of losing the empirical mind-mode while remaining immersed in the pure awareness of non-dual Consciousness.[2] The element of effortlessness and spontaneity here in contrast to the *nirodha* method is that the mind and the sense organs are seen as merely superimpositions on non-dual *Brahman* or Pure Consciousness rather than as separate vehicles which the *sādhaka* must bring under control in order to attain spiritual experience.[3] The mind being free from all its modes and states does not lose itself, but becomes the fearless *Brahman*, pure all-pervading Consciousness. It is on the basis of this philosophical understanding rooted in meditative experience that Advaita states that there is no practice or practices by which the Self can be realized. Śaṅkara's commentaries on *MK* III. 36, 39 and 47 make this quite clear. While there is the concession to the utility and even the necessity of practices, this is only granted when speaking from within the perspective of dualism, for one cannot speak as such from the non-dual position.[4]

1. *MK* III. 46.
2. *MK* III. 34 and 35.
3. See Śaṅkara's commentary on *MK* III. 39-40.
4. These verses which deny practice are declared from the highest condition of non-duality and as such of necessity deny any practice of any sort. For example, Śaṅkara in his commentary on *MK* III. 36 states, "With regard to this *Brahman* of such characteristics there can be no ceremony (practice), as others have, e.g. concentration of mind etc. that are different from the nature of the Self. The idea is this : As *Brahman* is by nature eternally pure, intelligent, and free, there can be no possibility of anything to be done in any way whatsoever, after the destruction of ignorance." In his commentary on *MK* III. 39 Śaṅkara adds, "for those to whom the mind and the sense-organs

7. The Modus Operandi of Asparśa-Yoga

> When the mind ceases to think as a consequence of the realisation of the Truth that is the Self, then the mind attains the state of not being the mind; in the absence of things to be perceived, it becomes a non-perceiver.
> —*MK* III.32

As the above verse indicates, the realization of the Truth that is the Self (*ātmasatya-anubodha*) is the goal of Gauḍapāda's *advaita sādhanā*. This awakening is said by Śaṅkara to be the result of following the instructions of scripture and the teacher.[1] The practice of these culminates in *nirvikalpa samādhi*[2] where the mind attains the state of ceasing to be the mind (*amanastā*[3] or *amanībhāva*).[4] When this occurs knowledge (*jñāna*) becomes established in the Self and the condition of liberation accrues for the successful seeker.

The process through which this condition is actualized, Gauḍapāda refers to as *manasaḥ nigraha* (control of the mind). This is the Advaitic *nididhyāsana* process of meditation or contemplation. Alike other meditative techniques, this practice is essentially an act of detaching the mind from the senses and concentrating it upon an internal object. During the actual

etc., that are imagined like a snake on a rope, have no existence in reality when considered apart from their essence that is *Brahman*—for those who have become identified with *Brahman*—comes fearlessness; and for them naturally is accomplished the ever-lasting peace called emancipation that is not dependent on any other factor, as we declared earlier . . . ." Finally he states on *MK* III. 47-48 that, "All such ideas—e.g. the control of the mind and so on, creation resembling the evolution of forms from earth and gold, and meditation—have been spoken as means leading to the realisation of the supreme Reality as It is in Itself; but these have not been spoken of as supremely true in themselves. The absolutely highest Truth, however, is : no individual being whichsoever, that is a doer or an enjoyer is born by any means whatsoever. Hence for the Self that is naturally unborn and non-dual there does not exist any source or cause for undergoing birth."

1. Śaṅkara on *MK* III. 32.
2. *MK* III. 32-34 and 37.
3. *MK* III. 32.
4. *MK* III. 31.

practice of meditation, the mind is to have only a purely internal function wherein the senses or the outer functions do not enter at all. The internal function of the mind can be of several kinds. While other kinds of meditation are upon "objects" of different sorts, the Advaitic meditation is strictly upon the Self (*ātman*). Meditation on the Self, being neither a point nor an object but the existential subject, thus appears to be a difficult task as it is quite unlike a technique involving concentration on some object which the subjective mind may grasp. This is the essential difference between the earlier *upāsanās* on *Oṅkāra* and the higher meditation on the *mātrā*-less aspect which represents *Turīya*. It is this more profound meditative task which Gauḍapāda ultimately sets for the *sādhaka*.

Meditation, then, is strictly speaking, an act wherein the mind alone is involved. The goal of meditation is to control the mind and bring it to the condition of equipoise (*samaprāptam*) which Gauḍapāda also calls the condition of "non-mind" (*amanībhāva*) wherein the Self alone remains as pure experience and knowledge.

The nature or quality of the mind is *vikalpa*, the production of thought forms, while the goal of meditation is to quell this incessant thought-flow in order to realize the Self upon which they subsist. The process is sometimes referred to as changing the direction of the mind, or further, as using the effects called thoughts to reach the source or cause of them. These ideas simply refer to the use of the mind functions themselves to go beyond the entire thought process. It is thus the utilization of the very cause of bondage or suffering to free itself.

The particular method to accomplish this is the *mantra*. Constant repetition by the mind of an idea is called *anusandhāna*.[1] It has the effect of linking the wandering mind to the desired object to the exclusion of other intrusions. The particular *Advaita* method is termed *ātma-anusandhāna* wherein the meditator constantly dwells on the Self.[2] Though there are several traditional *mokṣa-mantras* related to the *mahāvākyas* of the *Upaniṣads*,

1. Swāmī Bhoomananda Tirtha, *Brahma Vidya Abhyasa*, I (Trichur : Narayanasrama Thapovanam, 1970) pp. 92-95.

2. *MK* II. 36 and III. 43.

Gauḍapāda utilizes the sacred symbol *OM* for this purpose here. In this way he remains consistent with the scriptural source to which his text is appended and to the peculiar techniques known and current during his lifetime.

The consistent practice of *ātma-anusandhāna* first results in the lessening of intrusions of other thought forms, particularly those relating to the body and the world. The intense repetition of this *mantra* is necessary though it is repeated slowly and gently. This is still within the realm of *sparśa* or duality and not beyond it. While doing this practice the meditator is still "touching" as it were, the thought relating to the Self, the mind being the agency employed for this purpose. The goal is quite different from this, so the mind is then to be led in such a way that the *anusandhāna* itself ceases gradually and all thoughts and duality dissolve and disappear. When the *mantra* itself vanishes and with that all the thinking functions also, there is no duality and the non-dual Self remains. Though the processes within duality are made use of in meditation, the ideal aimed at is not the preservation of that process but the transcending of it and the attainment of the non-dual condition.[1] In this condition there is not "contact" (*sparśa*) with duality but rather the actualization of *Turiya*, "the fourth" beyond the three states of duality. For this reason it is called *Asparśa Yoga* by Gauḍapāda.

In order to do this Gauḍapāda advocates a specific attitude of mind. Once practice is undertaken the *sādhaka* is exhorted to continuously think of non-duality (*yojayet smṛtim advaite*).[2] The *anusandhāna* is part of this attitude. This fixation is to permeate all of the *sādhaka's* activities. The *sādhaka* must be diligent in his practice, showing no depression but exhibiting untiring effort.[3] The normal state of the mind is that it remains dispersed amidst the objects of desire and enjoyment which needs to be countered at every turn.[4]

Gauḍapāda states two maxims to further develop the necessary frame of mind for fruitful *sādhanā*.[5] In the first he advocates that by "constantly remembering that everything is full of misery,

1. Swāmi Bhoomananda Tirtha, *Brahma Vidya Abhyasa*, II, p. 89.
2. *MK* II. 36.
3. *MK* III. 41. This is called *abhyāsa* in the later tradition.
4. *MK* III. 42.
5. These are both given in *MK* III. 43.

one should withdraw the mind from the enjoyment arising out of desire." Turn the mind back from enjoyments remembering that the pleasures are not free from pain and misery. This is to counteract the natural propensity of the mind to seek external pleasurable experience through the vehicle of the senses. For this is based on the belief that the sense-objects are real, permanent, and that they can give happiness. Advaita says that these are false values superimposed through ignorance by the mind onto the sense-objects. Gauḍapāda thus asks the *sādhaka* to be ever vigilant and non-attached. Śaṅkara in his commentary on this verse affirms that this refers to the development of the spirit of dispassion or renunciation (*vairāgya*). This verse also refers to the process of *vicāra* or enquiry wherin the *sādhaka* revamps his life-style through the practice of discrimination (*viveka*) which aids detachment. *Viveka* should be the constant companion of spiritual life and practice according to Advaita. At every step of the way it is necessary and nonetheless so in meditative practice as shall be shown below.

The second piece of advice supplements the first. Gauḍapāda suggests that by "always remembering the fact that the birthless *Brahman* is everything, one does not perceive the born (i.e., duality)." This again affirms the need for the constant reflection on non-duality. It also affirms that while participating amidst the phenomenal universe, the perception of duality is delusory and the truth or reality of this very world is really non-duality. It is this theoretical understanding which must be eventually brought into actual direct experiential knowledge.

In this same verse Gauḍapāda points out the basic obstacle to Self-realization which the seeker is trying to overcome. Simply re-iterated, this is the basic misperception of Reality as duality which is caused by desire. The mind snared in this delusory dual framework participates in the subject-object, enjoyer-enjoyed structuring of existence. This is why Gauḍapāda says that the great obstacle for practising *yogis* is fear (*bhaya*) even though there is no real ground for such a reaction.[1] *Asparśa*

---

1. *MK* III.39.

Yoga is a lofty goal but most seekers are deterred by their fear of ego-loss. The thought that this *yoga* involves the disintegration of their own individuality arouses in them the fear of the destruction of the personality. According to Advaita, the true nature of the individual is his identity with the non-dual *Brahman* and the idea of individual existence is due to ignorance of one's own nature. *Brahman* is fearlessness itself, for it is ever-free, ever-illumined; there is nothing else of which it can be afraid. Fear comes from the sense of duality. This situation thus reflects the dual structure of existence and the role of the mind in its maintenance.

While all of this refers to the essential obstacle to overcome, Gauḍapāda points out some of the more specific variations of these that occur during the practice of the process of meditation itself. The four major categories are *laya* (un-consciousness), *vikṣepa* (distraction), *kaṣāya* (latent desire) and *sukha* (happiness). Gauḍapāda lists the obstacles as the seeker experiences them during meditative practice and following each gives advice or methods to counter each problem.[1] In so doing he also leads the aspirant progressively through the proper method of meditation which actualizes *Brahma-vidyā*, the experiential knowledge of Ultimate Reality.

The most recurrent obstacle in meditation, especially at the beginning of practice, is *vikṣepa* (distraction).[2] This is, in essence, the normal state of the mind interrupting the *ātma-anusandhāna*. The focussed mind loses its concentration when the *anusandhāna* is displaced by some other thoughts. Even when the practice appears smooth and easy, the deflection can occur unawares. By the time the meditator recognizes the intrusion of other thoughts, a period of time will have already elapsed. This is said to occur due to the habitual nature of the mind's working. It is difficult to change. The mental process is traced back to the *vāsanās* or desires which almost unconsciously propel the individual into habitual modes of action. Gauḍapāda states that the *sādhaka* should simply bring the dispersed or turbulent mind back to the *ātma-anusandhāna* practice and proceed to make it

1. *MK* III. 42 and 44-46.
2. *MK* III. 42 and 44.

tranquil again. This must be repeated over and over again untiringly. The mental attitudes of dispassion and discrimination which are being simultaneously developed will also aid this disciplining of the mind.

The next obstacle to the highest meditative experience is called *laya* (unconsciousness).[1] *Laya* suggests dissolution, absorption, sleep and other states of mind which are characterized by withdrawal from the awareness of external objects. Gauḍapāda uses the the term here in the sense of deep sleep (*suṣupti*) or yogic *samādhi*.[2] Gauḍapāda warns the meditator that such a state of experience is a major obstacle to the realization of truth. It is said to be as harmful as desire is in the finding of true freedom. During this state of *laya* there is no knowledge, it is an all-forgetful condition. There is the loss of awareness or consciousness, which characterizes the highest state. On this basis *laya* is regarded as useless. Further, like *suṣupti* (deep sleep) the *vāsanās* or latent desires are not attenuated but merely lie dormant awaiting re-awakening. While this state is peaceful and pleasant and is characterized by the absence of the subject-object relationship, it is not the highest non-dual experience. The ultimate aim of all spiritual practices is not the experience of oblivion but rather the realization of the true nature of the Self.

1. *MK* III. 42 and 44.

2. *Laya* has been considered to be different states of mental inactivity by various commentators within the tradition. Sadānanda explains it as *nidrā* (sleep). Madhusūdana refers to it as the pseudo-sleep states caused by such things as indigestion, over-eating, fatigue, etc. A modern exponent explains it thus : "*Laya* is almost similar to sleep (*sushupti*). But there is a clear difference between the two. I should say *laya* is denser and deeper than sleep. Usually when one goes asleep, the erect body will fall flat. But during *laya* this need not be so. Suppose you are sitting in meditation and *laya* takes place, you will continue to be in the same pose. When the condition breaks off you can find yourself in the same sitting pose. You will feel that you were in a state of absence, the mind and consciousness being absolutely devoid of all functions. There will be a lot of freshness and release coming to you after you break away. It will take some time (a few minutes) for you to rise up from your pose and proceed to walk or speak. Is *laya* then something like sleep? When you wake up from sleep there will be some drowsiness following. No such drowsiness will be there when you wake up from *laya*. On the basis of this difference you can distinguish them." Swāmī Bhoomananda Tirtha, *op cit.*, II, pp. 26-27.

To counter-act this situation, Gauḍapāda suggests that when the mind is merged in this kind of *samādhi* the meditator should awaken it again and continue with the original practice. Śaṅkara in his commentary adds that the practice of discrimination and detachment will aid in clarifying the difference between this state and the realization of the Self.[1]

Laya and *vikṣepa* are the two major obstacles which Gauḍapāda dwells on at length. The next obstacle, *kaṣāya*, is also portrayed as an experience or condition experienced during meditation. Similar to *laya*, it can also be erroneously taken as the supreme experience of *samādhi*. Gauḍapāda says that the meditator "should know when the mind is tinged with desire (*kaṣāya*)."[2] This is an intermeditate state, according to the commentator Śaṅkara, which must be differentiated from the desired condition of equipoise (*samaprāptam*).[3] This deceptive state has been called *stabdhībhāva* wherein the mind "becomes stiffened" and there is neither *laya* nor *vikṣepa*.[4] Due to this the mind cannot be fixed on the object of meditation. The cause of this condition, which is often by itself used to describe it, is *kaṣāya* or latent desire. This is the singular term for the classical passions of *rāga* (desire), *dveṣa* (hatred), *moha* (delusion), and *bhaya* (fear). The mind of the meditator in this intermediate condition is said to be under their influence and these remain in their latent form to re-activate and re-emerge upon awakening. The meditator has not yet realized his Self and Śaṅkara suggests that the *sādhaka* should again with diligence move the mind towards equipoise or equilibrium.

When meditation progresses and the mind gets used to concentration, it will experience unusual delights. Various forms of delightful experiences and happiness naturally accrue to the

---

1. Śaṅkara on *MK* III. 44.
2. *MK* III. 44.
3. It should be noted that although Śaṅkara states that this is an intermediary state and scholars have related it to classical meditative experiences, Gauḍapāda himself gives no directions to counter this as he does with all of the others. This description may indeed be only an analytical interpretation of the cause of the obstacles to meditation.
4. Karmarkar, *op. cit.*, p. 106 and Bhattacharya, *op. cit.*, p. 78.

meditator periodically. These by their nature will be alluring and hence the meditator will develop a tendency to experience them over and over again. This is why Gauḍapāda warns the *sādhaka* not to seek pleasure (*sukha*), not to take these delights as true spiritual experience, nor indulge in them when they arise. The joys and allurements of meditative experiences are thus the next obstacle discussed by Gauḍapāda.[1] Not only has he said that the propensity for enjoying the normal outer pleasures of the worldly life is a bondage to be removed through renunciation, but now he also says that the desire to enjoy the inner psychical or spiritual pleasures is just as binding to the meditator, if not more so than the one to experience outer enjoyments. The attraction for feelings of joy, pleasure, or happiness (*sukha*) in meditation can thus become a major impediment to liberation and Self-realization.

Gauḍapāda warns the *sādhaka* to counter this new attachment or attraction to *sukha* by becoming unattached (*niḥsaṅga*) through discrimination (*prajñā*). By the exercise of continuing discernment and judgement this particular attachment, alike any other remnants of the dual notion of enjoyer and enjoyed, can be expunged. Śaṅkara comments on this process of discrimination (*viveka*) as follows : The meditator should be unattached by gaining knowledge through discrimination wherein he should think that whatever happiness is experienced is a creation of ignorance and thus it is false. Then the mind should be turned back or withdrawn from such experiences.

This practice which Gauḍapāda here calls *prajñā* (discrimination) is the later traditional *viveka* formula. It is a basic truth of Advaita that only when the mind is attached to a thing will it want to be associated with it repeatedly. If the mind is detached from it, that very detachment will act as a force to keep away from it. The meditator is to realize the uselessness of the particular attraction in relation to the goal of liberation or Self-realization and on that basis grow indifferent towards it each time it emerges until it ceases to appear at all. Even if it appears at all after a time, the meditator should be sufficiently

1. *MK* III. 45.

detached so that the object of attraction does not bind him. The strength to dismiss and to outgrow comes from *viveka*, the intelligent assessment of the merits and demerits of the particular situation in regard to the final goal. Thus detachment can be cultivated through consistent and continuous awareness and effort on the part of the ardent seeker.

All of the obstacles to successful meditation which Gauḍapāda categorizes in his *Māṇḍūkya Kārikā* must be met and successfully overcome. The practice of discrimination (*prajñā* or *viveka*) is of prime importance. Using knowledge based on the new valuation of *sat* (truth), the *sādhaka* can judge the usefulness or uselessness of a particular situation in regard to achieving his goal. When one is convinced that something is useless, the desire for it decreases and eventually disappears. The conviction and recognition that it is not desirable and that it should not be indulged in, if preserved throughout *sādhanā*, will act as a safeguard against it. The whole matter thus simply calls for a clear analysis and understanding of any situation.

Advaita goes so far as to equate success in attaining Self-realization to this practice of discrimination alone. It is considered a *sine qua non* of spiritual practice. This is where *Advaita sādhanā* primarily differs from other systems of spiritual practice. It says that at every stage the *sādhaka* has to question himself as to what is the aim which is to be constantly kept in mind and whether that aim is being fulfilled, and to what degree, by the efforts that he is making. This very questioning will itself increase the *sādhaka's viveka*. When *viveka* reaches its zenith, the knowledge of the Self is said to instantly dawn. Self-knowledge is thus said by Advaitic texts to be the outcome brought about by the development of *viveka* rather than by any other practice.[1]

---

1. This brings to light the confusion in the literature on Advaita Vedānta *sādhana* concerning the methods of practice. Some scholars say that there is no practice, others that the practice is meditation, and still others that it is the practice of discrimination exclusively. In a sense all are right to a certain degree. Some traditions of Advaita do not advocate meditative practices while others do. Each *guru* also takes a certain unique position in regards to these different possibilities. Nonetheless, Gauḍapāda and the soteriological practices he enunciates in his *Māṇḍūkya Kārikā* clearly define a meditative process wherein the practice of discrimination is given a prominent role.

After all these obstacles have been conquered and the state of steadiness (*niścalatva*) becomes experienced however fleetingly, there is yet another impediment to realization which occurs. Even when the mind becomes periodically stilled and remains established in steadiness it tends to revert to its former condition of agitation and externality.[1] This is due to the persistence of the mind's outgoing propensities.

There are two important points made here. The first concerns the periodic success the meditator has in regard to collecting and concentrating the mind. Freed of the other obstacles the mind is led to a state of stillness and steadiness which is thought-free, emotion-free and vibration-free. Initially these periods do not last long and the *sādhaka* must again rally his energies to overcome this problem. As Gauḍapāda points out, the mind should again be collected and applied to the concentration on the *anusandhāna*. This is not an easy task and thus the re-iteration that the meditator must try hard with diligence until the mind becomes as still as the unflickering flame of a candle in a windless place.[2]

Though the mind at times attains equipoise or equilibrium which is the achievement of the *samādhi* state, this must yet be stabilized. Eventually this becomes an easy transition. The ability to stay in that condition for long periods of time effortlessly is to be worked for at this stage. This alone is said to bring success, for it is this non-dual experience which is to be fully actualized and the results of which are to eventually permeate the *sādhaka's* entire life-style.

Thus, even after glimpses of the highest state are attained and this state is becoming easier to achieve and the periods of steadiness are lengthened, there is still work to be done by the *sādhaka*. Traditionally, this latter aspect is called *vāsanā-kṣaya*, the destruction or attenuation of desire in the form of impressions, habits or tendencies within the individual's personality. This is the second important point made in this part of the verse.

What then is the nature of the highest meditative condition, this *samādhi* which Gauḍapāda eulogizes in his *Māṇḍūkya Kārikā*? This *nirvikalpa samādhi* state is defined as the ideal state and

1. M*K*. III. 45.
2. *MK* III. 45 and 46 with Śaṅkara's commentary.

described by different psychological terms. The mind becomes "motionless" (*aniṅgana, niścalā sthitiḥ*).[1] This is in contrast to the mind's normal agitated and discursive state. The mind neither becomes lost in sleep or trance, nor dispersed amidst the objects of perception, nor does it appear in the form of objects.[2] The mind is "non-mind" or "steady" (*niścala*).[3] It is truly "equipoised" or in "equilibrium" (*samaprāpta*).[4] It is *śānta*, "tranquil" or at peace, in the sense wherein Gauḍapāda talks metaphorically of the "quietude" of the fire-brand in its real non-dual condition.[5] Because of these characteristics it is called *amanastā* or *amanībhāva*, "non-mind"[6] since it ceases to have the qualities associated with the discursive mind. The empirical mind ceases to act, i.e., there is no agitation (*spandana*), no imagination (*saṅkalpa*), no thinking (*cintā*), etc. It "turns back" (*vinivartate*) from the objects of the dual world.[7] Having no relation at all with the objects of duality the mind or consciousness is said to be in a condition of "sameness" or "non-differentiation" (*sāmya*).[8] The mind "rests in itself" (*svastha*)[9] having "become identified with *Brahman*" (*niṣpannam brahma*)[10] and is thus "liberated" (*sanirvāṇa*).[11] The substrate Consciousness is exposed and realized in its fullness and profundity.[12]

1. *MK* III. 46 and IV, 80.
2. *MK* III. 46.
3. *MK* III. 45.
4. *MK* III. 44.
5. *MK* III. 47 and title of the fourth *prakaraṇa*.
6. *MK* III. 31 and 32.
7. *MK* III. 46 and IV. 79-80.
8. *MK* III. 38, IV. 80, 95 and 100.
9. *MK* III. 47.
10. *MK* III. 46.
11. *MK* III. 47.
12. "It would be wrong to regard this mode of being of the Spirit as a simple "trance" in which consciousness was emptied of all content. Non-differentiated entasis is not "absolute emptiness." The "state" and the "knowledge" simultaneously expressed by this term refer to a total absence of objects in consciousness, not to a consciousness absolutely empty. For, on the contrary, at such a moment consciousness is saturated with a direct and total intuition of being." Eliade, *op. cit.*, p. 93.

Mind or Consciousness is birthless (*aja*), non-dual (*advaya*) and beyond description (*akathya*) in this condition.[1]

This highest state is the experiential realization or knowledge of what is variously described as the Self (*ātman*), *Brahman*, *Turīya*, and Pure Consciousness (*citta*). Meditatively it is a unique state or condition of "still awareness" which is quite different from the other states of consciousness. Rather than a union with the objects of dual experience it is a mergence with the subject of all experience. It is a state of "self-cognition" wherein the mind stands cognizing its own essence. This is pure consciousness or awareness. There is no "other" here. In the *samādhi* condition of stillness and peacefulness of mind, the consciousness present in it is similar to that of deep sleep (*suṣupti*). It is like what a person feels during sleep. But unlike sleep, this stillness is recognized and experienced by the mind in its current awareness at that time. As awareness here is ever present and available to experience, it is quite opposed to the sleep state, for the knowledge of sleep comes to the individual only in the form of a memory after awakening. Again, it is similar to the waking state in that there is no absence of awareness. But just as the meditator is aware of the state of wakefulness, so will he be aware of the *samādhi* condition even when he is within it.[2] In fact, Advaita states that it is only in this "fourth" condition that one can truly come to know and realize one's true nature as pure consciousness which is one's own essence or Self.

---

1. MK III. 47 and IV. 80.

2. For this description see Swāmi Bhoomananda Tirtha, *BVA*, Vol. II, pp. 66-67, 71 and 81. In summation he states, "for the purpose of description, we can say that it is a kind of sleep during which you are able to feel, Yes, I am asleep. In other words, it is a wakeful slumber or sleepy wakefulness. This is the reason for my saying that the Yoga state is akin to sleep and also opposed to it at the same time. The akinness is on the ground of its peaceful stillness and opposedness on the ground of the presence of awareness. Thus the dawning of the Yoga state or the setting in of the spiritual stillness (*samādhi*) will be a feature quite natural and pleasant. It will be like the setting in of sleep at the end of wakefulness. Or like the dawning of wakefulness at the end of a refreshing sleep. Or like the emergence of a thought in the mind following the subsidence of another." (pp. 81 and 83).

8. Self-Realization

That highest Bliss is located in one's own Self. It is quiescent, coexistent with liberation, beyond description, and birthless. And since It is identical with the unborn knowable (*Brahman*), they call It the Omniscient (*Brahman*).
—*MK* III. 47

This experience of non-duality Gauḍapāda calls the "realization of the truth of the Self" (*ātmasatyānubodha*).[1] The final test in Advaita Vedānta is this experience. The end or goal of *Brahma-vijñāna*, the enquiry into the nature of reality, is *anubhava* or immediate knowledge (*aparokṣa-jñāna*). Realization is truly seeing or perceiving (*dṛś*) and understanding or knowing Reality firsthand.[2] It is knowledge (*jñāna*) which is *akalpa*, non-conceptual or devoid of all imagination. It is said to be non-different from the knowable (*jñeyābhinna*) which is *Brahman*.[3] *Brahman* is the sole object of knowledge. *Brahman*, as realized by the individual in meditation, is non-different from the Self (*ātman*).[4]

Gauḍapāda in his *Kārikā* equates this realization with the path of knowledge (*jñāna mārga*). The path to perfection (*vaiśāradya*)[5] lies in and through *jñāna*, for Ignorance which is the root of all the imperfections and ills of the world can be destroyed only by corrective knowledge. Thus knowledge is held by Gauḍapāda

1. *MK* III. 32.
2. *MK* II. 35 and 38.
3. *MK* III. 33 and IV. 1.
4. The exact equivalence may not seem possible yet there is said to be a relation of some principle, such as Consciousness, within the individual that is present everywhere as the substratum of all experience. It is the fundamental experience of the identity of being on both the individual and universal levels. A good summary statement is found in Deutsch, *op. cit.*, p.56. "The Self is one, it is not different from *Brahman*. This is the central meta-religious or meta-psychological affirmation of Advaita Vedānta. It means that man is essentially spiritual; that in the most profound dimension of his being he is no longer the "individual" that he ordinarily takes himself to be, but that he is precisely Reality itself. The affirmation is based not on mere speculation, but upon experience supported by a phenomenological analysis of what we erroneosly take to be our selves. For Advaita, to affirm oneself as Reality is an act of a free man. The knowledge of non-difference leads to freedom, to the realization of the potentialities of our human being."
5. *MK* IV. 94.

to be the direct means to release.[1] Again, this *jñāna* is not an intellectual understanding but the direct personal apprehension or experience which has been indicated above.[2]

This existential grasp of reality is described by Gauḍapāda in two ways. Upon knowing the truth, the *jñāni*, the realized man, becomes one with the Absolute Reality. This reflects the traditional dictum, that to "know" *Brahman* is to "become" *Brahman*. As such this experience partakes of the characteristics attributed to *Brahman*. *Brahman* is said to be unborn and eternal (*brahma jñeyam ajaṁ nityam*),[3] non-dual (*advaya*),[4] homogeneous (*sama*),[5] all-pervading (*vyāpi*),[6] self-established (*svastha*),[7] peace (*śānta*),[8] ever-luminous (*sakṛt-vibhāta*),[9] all-knowledge (*sarvajña*),[10] free from limitations (*akārpaṇyam*),[11] the nature of supreme happiness (*sukham anuttamam*) and release (*sanirvāṇa*),[12] though ultimately *Brahman* is really said to be indescribable as it is without name (*anāmakam*) and form (*arūpakam*).[13] This description presents a rather abstract conception of the condition of liberation. It attempts to characterize this supersensuous and supramental experience in which the illusory notions of name and form, subject and object, etc. completely disappear.

Although abstract, these terms are really only the intellectual expression of a concrete religious experience which can become

---

1. *MK* III. 33, 38, 47, IV.1, 88, 89, 96 and 99.
2. That the "object" of knowledge is said to be unrealizable or unknowable through thought further indicates the necessity of adopting a non-rational technique of piercing through the subject-object relationship to experience the non-relational Subject. Thus the unique meditative technique of *Asparśa Yoga*.
3. *MK* III. 2, 33, IV. 77 and 91-93.
4. *MK* IV. 45 and 77.
5. *MK* III. 2, 38 and IV. 77.
6. *MK* III. 3 (with Śaṅkara's commentary) especially when compared to *ākāśa*.
7. *MK* III. 47.
8. *MK* III. 47 and IV. 45.
9. *MK* III. 36, IV. 81 and 91-93.
10. *MK* III. 36.
11. *MK* III. 2, IV. 81 and 91-93.
12. *MK* III. 47.
13. *MK* II. 36.

intelligible upon further examination. Take the concept of "omniscience" (*sarvajñatā*) as an example here.[1] This term is used to differentiate the normal state of knowledge or knowingness from the new condition of enlightenment. This state of omniscience accrues only when the *sādhaka* has transcended the narrow limits of human knowledge and has identified with his *Ātman*. *Sarvajñatā* is an attribute of *Ātman* or *Brahman*. This condition of "all-knowledge" is the "Knowledge Absolute" of later Vedāntic writings. It represents the superconscious condition of the Self as pure Consciousness, the eternal Witness who is the knower of all things at all times and in all places. The successful seeker becomes one with this upon realization. Rather than suggesting that he is now the knower of all things past, present, and future, it purports that the enlightened man "shares" this consciousness which is the substratum of all knowledge. He continuously abides in that new condition and understanding. Though personal, this realm of experience is not exclusive to him, nor does he partake of its universality except in that he is now conjoined with it through the experience of it as his essential being and as the vehicle of all knowledge. Every form of experience and knowledge comes from or through this Consciousness. It is this underlying essence or ground upon which the objects of experience manifest. It is the real bestower and possessor of all knowledge. The Self-realized man experiences and constantly abides in this source of all knowledge. This full realization is said to be permanent and the seeker is never again subject to false knowledge or misapprehension of Reality. This is why the Vedāntic texts state that when *Brahman* is known, nothing else needs to be known.

The second description of the state of liberation supplements the first one which enumerates some of the characteristics of *Brahman*. It helps to give a clearer picture of the psycho-spiritual condition of the *sādhaka* who has attained illumination. Release means the end or destruction of misery (*saṃsāra* or *duḥkha*) and the attainment of fearlessness and eternal peace and bliss.[2] Take "fearlessness" as an illustration here as the others have been

1. *MK* III. 47, IV. 84, 85 and 89.
2. *MK* I. 10, 29, III. 40 and 47.

previously described. In *MK* IV. 78, Gauḍapāda declares that the seeker attains the state of fearlessness (*abhayam padam*) which is free from sorrow and desire.[1] Gauḍapāda emphasizes fear as a basic factor of our existence and relation to the world before liberation. This use of "fear" as a basic concept exemplifying the bound condition of man is upaniṣadic in origin. Gauḍapāda quotes the traditional *rāga-bhaya-krodha* formula in *MK* II. 35 for example. In one of his main verses concerning *Asparśa Yoga*, *MK* III. 39, he emphatically relates this idea of "fear" to individuality or the ego-sense and all of its concomitant problems. Fear is the individual's greatest enemy as it mars every aspect of one's life.[2] The condition of freedom, on the other hand, is that of *Brahman* described as a state or condition of "fearlessness." The enlightened man becomes fearless, having no desires and nothing to lose. Being thus he also finds peace and bliss as suffering and pain have been overcome. This is the psycho-spiritual transformation of bound man into the condition of freedom.

The liberated man sees and experiences both himself and the world differently than before. A transvaluation process has occurred. The *jñāni* undergoes an axio-noetic change wherein the self (subject) and the world (object) are no longer valued as before. They in fact are said to lose their value entirely as separate entities. The Self is realized as one and non-different from *Brahman* and only this can now be given the highest valuation. All else appears shallow and false when seen in this light. Thus the world seen dualistically is totally devalued. That is why Gauḍapāda uses the expression of dream, illusion, etc. to indicate and describe the world now seen from this new

---

1. Also mentioned in *MK* I. 25.

2. "In enjoyment, there is the fear of disease; in social position, the fear of falling-off; in wealth, the fear of hostile kings; in honour, the fear of humiliation; in power, the fear of foemen; in beauty, the fear of old age; in scriptural erudition, the fear of opponents; in virtue, the fear of traducers; in body, the fear of death. All things of this world pertaining to man are attended with fear; renunciation alone stands for fearlessness." (Bhartṛhari, *Vairāgya-Śatakam*, verse 31). Fear is not taken in its limited sense of the emotion called fright but incorporates all of man's agitations, desires, passions and hopes wherein frustration or losss can occur.

perspective. He speaks from the highest viewpoint (*paramārtha satya*) and as such he classifies the dual world as unreal when compared to the standpoint of the Reality which is one without a second. The world of difference is but a dream for the *jñāni* while it remains the conventional reality for all others. Gauḍapāda uses the conventional distinctions for the purpose of teaching and raising the ignorant to such an understanding. It is not his purpose to establish the doctrine of *māyā* as the final truth but to lead the mind of the aspirant to the knowledge of *Brahman*, the non-dual reality.[1]

The world is sublated (*bādha*) as the later tradition terms it. This is to distinguish it from the cessation (*nivṛtti*) of the world. In the former the process is like the overcoming of the rope-snake illusion where nothing is transformed in the overcoming of the cosmic illusion of the *Brahman*-world distinction. The change which is brought about is only in the outlook and not in the object itself. The change in the realization of liberation is only epistemological and not ontological. It is not the transformation to a new realm of experience, but rather it involves a transvaluation of the existing one. It is not an attainment, nor a modification, nor a production *de novo* but rather a discovery of an already existing situation through the removal of primeval ignorance.[2]

Though this appears to be a form of spiritual negation in its denial and devaluation it is really the ultimate in affirmation. It would indeed be negative if it only said that the world did

1. "Does Vedānta really ask us to negate the world? Does it really teach us to negate the existing objects? A student of the *Kārikā* will at once realize that there is nothing to be negated or added. That which exists can never be non-existent. *Brahman* alone is existent on account of its persistence in all acts of cognition. Names, forms and relations are illusory on account of their changeability and negatability. Vedānta teaches us to realize the world as *Brahman* and then be one with it. Vedānta teaches us to see *Brahman* everywhere even in the so-called illusion. An illusion can never be real and it is perceived on account of our ignorance. A Vedāntist does not negate the world which, being *Brahman*, can never be negated. It only asks the student to know the real nature of the world." Swāmī Nikhilānanda, *op. cit.*, p. xxxi.

2. This is suggested consistently by Gauḍapāda. An example of this can be found in *MK* IV. 91-95.

not exist, but instead it is a positive orientation as it affirms the all-comprehensiveness of the non-dual Absolute. The *ātman* is not annihilated when the three states of consciousness are said to cease to exist. The seeker comes to realize the true nature of the Self and also how the whole universe follows from and is sustained by this absolute. To see everything and everybody as the one *Brahman* implies a perfect integration not experienced in the manifold universe which is based on the dual conception of separateness and individuality. Thus this experience, while indicating the non-ultimacy of mundane reality, affirms the ultimate nature of Reality as the Self (*ātman*) or *Brahman*.

The individual who undergoes this transforming experience of enlightenment and becomes a "liberated man" is called a "knower" (*jñāni*), though Gauḍapāda uses many synonymous terms to indicate this idea. The liberated man is referred to as a *manīṣi* (man of wisdom),[1] a *buddha* (enlightened man),[2] a *dhīra* (man of intelligence),[3] a *vidvān* (knower),[4] a *brāhmaṇa* (knower of *Brahman*),[5] and a *muni* (sage).[6]

This *muni* is a renunciate, a contemplative person, well versed in the Vedic literature and its profound teachings. He is said to be unafflicted by desire, fear and anger.[7] As a mendicant, or man of self-restraint he is above all praise and salutation, has no use for prayers to deities nor the sacrificial offerings to the ancestors (*pitṛs*) and other rituals, nor need he follow the *vidhi* (injunctions) or *niṣedha* (prohibitions) rules. His only supports should be the unchanging *Ātman* and the ever-changeful body-vehicle. As such he stays or wanders at will being dependent on circumstance for his physical needs.[8] To the world he appears as normal or dull-witted (*jaḍavat*) as he does not let others know

1. *MK* IV. 54.
2. *MK* IV. 80 and 99.
3. *MK* I. 28.
4. *MK* IV. 87.
5. *MK* IV. 85 and 86.
6. *MK* I. 29, II. 35 and 36.
7. *MK* II. 35.
8. *MK* II. 37.

what he has become.[1] This is the natural modesty and conduct of a *brāhmaṇa* (knower of *Brahman*).

Continuously meditating on and then abiding in that non-duality, the sage realizes the truth of the Self and the world. The Self is beyond all thought constructions, ever free and non-dual and the world is seen to be free from the variegated diversity of the phenomenal world (*prapañcopaśama*).[2] Thus realizing the truth inward and outward he remains unmoved from it. Becoming identified with that Reality he thereafter derives his pleasures from it alone and takes care to see that he does not deviate from that until his body comes to an end.[3]

This is the dynamic spiritual condition of *jīvanmukti* (liberation while alive).[4] Gauḍapāda says that the liberated man does not revert to the dual plane of consciousness. The idea here is that those who have realized this state of consciousness are never again subject to false knowledge which is described futher as the misapprehension of Reality.[5] In practical terms this means that the realized man upon return to the field of active life in the three states of consciousness is not affected by the world-play around him.[6] Firmly established in his own Self, serene and confident, filled with bliss, possessing creative strength and power, he enjoys life but is completely detached. While the ordinary man is tossed hither and thither by

1. *MK* II. 36. The term *jaḍavat* literally means dull, senseless, stupid, irrational, unintelligent or inanimate. It usually refers to a person who is dull-witted, simple-minded, or idiotic. Often such a designation is used to describe a realized being to distinguish him from other men. It can refer to his seemingly unconventional ideas and behaviour which reflects his new condition on one extreme of interpretation. Or, on the other hand as Śaṅkara suggests in the commentary, it refers to the fact that though the Self-realized man is different he abides within the society of other men who in comparison to the liberated condition are rather *jaḍa*-like. Living in this fashion the sage does not flaunt his new understanding but appears like all others when mixing in society.

2. *MK* II. 35.

3. *MK* II. 38.

4. This term is not used in the text but is indicated in *MK* I. 5, II. 35-38, IV. 85-86 and 89. This is also indicated by the term *jaḍavat* in II. 36.

5. *MK* IV. 46.

6. *MK* I. 5.

the play of opposites and the passions of the finite self, he is unmoved by these and is not involved on a personal ego level. Because his ego-hood has been subdued in him and replaced, as it were, by his true Self with which he is now identified, the world no longer touches him.[1] He experiences the world from a condition of perfect detachment which, Gauḍapāda says, is the result of the natural humility and tranquillity of the non-dual awakening.[2] The liberated man is naturally restrained or self-controlled and at peace as he partakes of the equipoise of *Brahman* with which he is firmly identified and established.[3]

Being a rigorous non-dualist, Gauḍapāda maintains that once liberation is attained there is in effect no actor, no action, nor object to be acted upon. This is the logical conclusion from such a premise. But he does indicate in his description of the *jīvanmukta* condition that the emancipated man does act, though in a new way.[4] This point is summarized as follows:

> It is possible to do any work which always implies the triad of perceiver, perceived, and perception, if one be established in non-dual *Brahman*. The idea may involve a logical or psychological contradiction, but this position can be fully justified from the metaphysical or rather, philosophical standpoint. One pursuing Truth disinterestedly, when once established in Truth, can see this world of multiplicity and at the same time know it to be the non-dual *Brahman*, pure, free, and ever-illumined. A knower of Truth moves and acts in the world like an ordinary man. He feels hungry and thirsty. He goes to sleep when tired. He feels compassion

1. This is the definition of the successful practitioner of *Asparśa Yoga* in *MK* III. 38 and IV. 2.

2. *MK* IV. 86.

3. The designation of *śama* (peacefulness) and *dama* (self-control) here resembles the list of the *ṣaṭ-sampatti* (six attainments) of later Vedānta which Gauḍapāda has indicated both here and in other verses. These six are : *śama* (mental tranquillity), *dama* (restraint), *uparati* (dispassion), *titikṣā* (endurance), *samādhāna* (intentness of mind) and *śraddhā* (faith). This list is one of the traditional four qualifications which also include *viveka* (discrimination), *vairāgya* (renunciation) and *mumukṣutva* (desire for liberation).

4. *MK* II. 32, then I. 9 and IV. 85.

> for the misery of others and tries his utmost to alleviate it; but at the same time he sees everywhere the non-dual *Brahman* alone, ever-free and ever-pure.[1]

This is a new mode of living. It is a non-action or non-egocentric living; a living and doing without desire. There is nothing to be done as there exists no doer. Yet this merely means that there is no doer in the conventional sense while action is being done. Every wish, craving, desire, all hope and fear have been destroyed for the liberated man. As Gauḍapāda says, "what can he desire who has everything ?"[2] For there is said to be no desirer nor object of desire when oneness with *Brahman* is realized. Thus Gauḍapāda describes the condition of Self-Realization which accrues for the successful aspirant upon becoming a true *Asparśa-yogin.*

In conclusion, Gauḍapāda sets out a complete spiritual regime within the pithy statements of his *Māṇḍūkya Kārikā.* Taken out of the context of the intimate *guru-śiṣya* (preceptor-disciple) relationship this text needs to be presented in this schematic fashion where the assumptions concerning the nature of human life, man's aspirations, and the detailed path of *sādhanā* are fully described. Once this is accomplished, Gauḍapāda's text can be seen and valued as it is within the tradition of Advaita Vedānta. There it is highly regarded as a philosophical treatise and particularly as a practical teaching text. Both of these aspects are soteriologically oriented and this purpose has been given prominence. Through this ultimate concern the disparate aspects of the texts are unified into a cohesive whole and the religio-spiritual dimension of the *Māṇḍūkya Kārikā* is clearly seen.

---

1. Swāmī Nikhilānanda, *op. cit.*, p. xxx.
2. *MK* I. 9.

Chapter VII

THE SYNTHESIS OF PHILOSOPHY AND RELIGION IN GAUḌAPĀDA'S *MĀṆḌŪKYA KĀRIKĀ*

Gauḍapāda's *Māṇḍūkya Kārikā* has been systematically presented to indicate the essential soteriological perspective of his teachings. This chapter will attempt to further indicate the inter-relationships of the various aspects of Gauḍapāda's philosophical and practical teachings under this purpose. First, the integral unity of the various components of the system of thought will be indicated. The concept of touch, contact, connection and relation will be used to indicate this unification. Secondly, a summary conclusion of the material presented in this work will be given.

1. The Integral Unity of Gauḍapāda's Māṇḍūkya Kārikā

The purpose of the present work has been to point out the essential soteriological concern and purpose of Gauḍapāda's teachings as expounded in the *Māṇḍūkya kārikā*. The term "teachings" is used here to indicate the underlying religio-spiritual dimensions of this text. For the text embodies several elements of the Indian soteriological quest. Philosophy, metaphysics, epistemology, psychology and religion are all blended under this essential concern. Intellectually, any component can be isolated and given prominence. This has been done by scholars who in general have particularly isolated the philosophical and metaphysical aspects of Gauḍapāda's thought to the relative neglect of his meta-psychology, the religio-spiritual quest and the means advocated to actualize this. The present work has focused on these latter aspects of the text in an attempt to clarify the nature of Gauḍapāda's teachings as well as to fulfil the need of fully describing this material which provides a more complete picture of Gauḍapāda and his *Māṇḍūkya kārikā*.[1] Though these various elements of the text can be separated, they are quite inter-related and reciprocally influence each other.

It is because of this that the major categorical conceptualizations of philosophy and religion are stated to be inter-twined. This premise has been summarized in Chapter III above; the remainder of this work being the detailed explication of this in a specific author and text within the tradition of Advaita Vedānta. This system is seen to be a synthesis of theory and practice, an enquiry into the nature of *Brahman* which is regarded as Ultimate Reality and a search for the path for the realization of *Brahman* regarded as the highest goal of life. The knowledge of the unity of *Ātman-Brahman* is the aim of philosophical thought and the goal of spiritual attainment in Advaita Vedānta as a whole and in Gauḍapāda as a particular example of this tradition. These two are but different aspects of the same attempt at realizing the highest end of life. Philosophy forms the theoretical base of religious or spiritual experience whereas religion makes possible the actualization of concrete spiritual experience. Each one is looking at the same problem, that of *mokṣa*, from different perspectives and in that sense each has a different and distinct function. The real bifurcation of not only philosophy and religion, but of the more minute elements of metaphysics, epistemology, psychology and religion are not found in Gauḍapāda's work to any great extent and it is only in the later more developed tradition that these are expressly isolated and precisely determined. In the *Māṇḍūkya Kārikā* they are spread throughout the work and clustered together when felt necessary to complete a point or argument. Much of

1. This mode of enquiry has been endorsed in Conio, *op.cit.*, p. 158:
"We have therefore to explore Gauḍapāda's various religious suggestions, so as to interpret his thought thoroughly. Inspite of the composite character of the *Kārikās*, a unification of his philosophy, besides the one made by Śaṅkara in his *bhāṣya* from a metaphysical angle, may also be made fruitfully from the religious-mystical standpoint."

the detail of each element is merely assumed when reading the text and yet each element can be discriminated and treated separately when the situational background is discerned.[1]

Gauḍapāda's metaphysic is presupposed in the text, drawing the teaching from traditional, principally Upaniṣadic sources. He assumes the truth of the *Brahman-Ātman* identity and its equation with *Turīya*. This Truth or Reality is said to be non-dual (*advaita*), a principle which he philosophically and logically treats throughout the text. The Absolute can be indicated in no other way, for it is indescribable in any known way. It is indeterminable as it both encompasses everything and goes beyond everything known. Though it is seemingly so ineffable it is said to remain as the only true reality. Once this is known, that which is experienced phenomenally as the multiple universe is seen to be merely the play of the pairs of opposites, the delusory or relative reality of *māyā*. The highest experience of Reality (*paramārtha satya*) is *avyavahārya*, i.e., non-relative, beyond empirical relations and conventional dealings. It is not dependent on, nor related to anything, to the other things of the world. It is literally unattached to, or untouched by, dual existence. Rather than being bound in the vacillations of the dual world, experiencing the endless round of *saṃsāra* and its essential *duḥkha* (frustration, suffering and pain), the individual experiencing and identified with this essential Being is said to experience and abide in true freedom (*mokṣa*), peace and bliss.

This non-dual Reality is treated philosophically by Gauḍapāda in his arguments concerning the concept of *ajātivāda* (non-origination). Reality known variously as *Ātman*, *Brahman*, *Turīya*, and *citta* is stated to be birthless and in no way given to manifestation except through *māyā*. This involves a critique of causality and an examinatian of the dependent relations of the dualistically conceived universe. To this Gauḍapāda turns his keen mind and makes an original contribution within the field of philosophy while at the same time keeping its soteriological purpose in view.

1. The differing perspective and functions of each have been systematically presented as follows : Philosophy and metaphysics in Chapters III and IV, epistemology in Chapter III, psychology in Chapter V, and the religio-spiritual aspects in Chapters III and VI in particular.

In the area of epistemology Gauḍapāda is consistent within his total system. He gives scripture (*śruti*)and traditional knowledge (*śabda*) a high place as valid sources of knowledge especially in his metaphysics. He uses these plus the commonly accepted *pramāṇas* of perception (*pratyakṣa*) and inference (*anumāna*) in his philosophical portions. And finally all of these are disvalued as *parokṣa* or mediate knowledge when compared to *anubhūti* or *anubhava*, direct personal intuitive experience. This is real *jñāna*, knowledge. It is *Ātma*-or *Brahma-vidyā*, the knowledg e or realization of the Truth that is the Self or Ultimate Reality.

This epistemology aspect is said to be experientially based. From this perspective Gauḍapāda introduces the idea of Consciousness (*citta*) as another vehicle for examining his propositions. Mind or Consciousness is shown to have different levels or modes of manifestation and experience. It is through this concept that Gauḍapāda brings his lofty metaphysic together with his practical religious or spiritual discipline. For he elaborates a meta-psychology which he utilizes to aid the explanation and elaboration of both these aspects. Consciousness is categorized into the basic aspects or modes of the outward or objective consciousness of the waking state, the inner or subjective sphere of the dream and alike states of consciousness, the un-consciousness of deep sleep-like states, and the condition of pure consciousness which underlies and yet transcends these other three states. This latter condition is described and defined consistently within Gauḍapāda's system of thought.

Gauḍapāda expands this into a psychological theory which becomes the basis of the meditative practice which he proposes. He equates Pure Consciousness with the "unborn" mind which he calls *amanastā* and *amanībhāva*, "non-mind". This highest condition is described variously in terms of the quietude of the mind, its motionlessness, its steadiness, equipoise or equilibrium. The mind ceases to have the qualities associated with the discursive mind. There is said to be no agitation, no imagination, nor thinking. It "turns back" fr om the objects of the dual world and thus having no rel ation with duality it is said to be in a condition of "sameness" or "non-differentiation" (*sāmya*). The substrate Consciousness is experienced in its fullness. Rather than a union with the objects of dual experience it is a mergence with the subject of all experience. It is a state of "self-cognition" wherein the mind stands cognizing its own essence. Resting in itself it becomes identified with the non-dual *Brahman* and is thus liberated.

Meditatively this is a unique condition of "still awareness" quite different from the other states of consciousness. It is called *nirvikalpa samādhi* from this religious or spiritual perspective. This is the esteemed experience which Gauḍapāda terms *Asparśa Yoga.* This is his designation for the unique non-dualist orientation to both the means and the goal of the spiritual quest. In the *Māṇḍūkya Kārikā* it becomes the pivotal concept of his soteriological concern.

The inter-relationship and inter-dependence of these various elements can be easily seen within each *prakaraṇa.* A number of key verses from any one of the *prakaraṇas* could be selected and when taken together would illustrate the integral unity of the *Māṇḍūkya Kārikā* within Gauḍapāda's soteriological concern. This, for example, can be done with the verses from the third *prakaraṇa* given in Appendix I or by using the verses selected from the fourth *prakaraṇa* given in Appendix II. These latter verses will be used here to briefly document this point. Each of the categories or perspectives will be shown to be integrally related around the concept of touch, contact, connection or relation.

From the standpoint of metaphysics, *Brahman, Ātmān,* or *Turīya* is stated to be *avyavahārya,* beyond relations or empirical connections.[1] It so transcends these categories that all that can be predicated of it is its essential nature as non-duality (*advaya* or *advaita*).[2] Philosophically, this absolute is said to be *aja,* unborn or birthless as it transcends relative or dependent causal connections or relations.[3] Epistemologically, the highest knowledge (*jñāna*) which is not mediate is stated to be non-relational since it has no objective relation as it does not reach out

1. *MUp.* 12.
2. *MK* IV. 100. Duality is partially defined in *MK* IV. 7 as the interdependent relation between two things which in this instance are the subject and object.
3. *MK* IV. 77-78, 83-84 and 100.

or extend to objects (*na kramate*).[1] It is completely *asaṅga* (unattached). Consciousness (*citta*) in its true state, from the perspective of Gauḍapāda's meta-psychology, is said to be non-dual (*advaya*), birthless (*aja*), and unattached (*asaṅga* or *niḥsaṅga*).[2] It has no contact (*na spṛśati* or *na saṃspṛśati*) with external objects in all the three states.[3] Gauḍapāda's spiritual practice or discipline is named *Asparśa Yoga*, which again reflects this soteriological goal or highest condition as being untouched, contactless, or free from relationships.[4] The practice of the technique or method of *Asparśa Yoga* leads the seeker to this condition of liberation which Gauḍapāda calls the state of fearlessness (*abhaya*).[5]

Gauḍapāda uses these key words to describe the common characteristic of the various perspectives. Through the concept of touch, contact, connection or relation designated by the use of several different terms, he indicates the integral unity of his work as a whole. Though seemingly, separate elements with differing functions, the perspectives of metaphysics, philosophy, epistemology, psychology, religion and spiritual discipline all come together when the terms used in the text are compared and found to be similar in meaning and indication. The two major terms here are *asaṅga* and *asparśa*. *Asaṅga* is used in *MK* III. 45, IV. 72,79, 96 and 97 to describe a religious practice and attitude, the nature of consciousness, the nature of knowledge, and in a reference to the concept of non-origination successively. The term *asparśa* or a form of the verb *spṛś* is used in *MK* III. 39, IV. 2, 26, 27 and 84 to successively indicate the goal of Advaita and the practical means to achieve that end,

1. *MK* IV. 96 and 99.
2. *MK* IV. 28, 72, 77, 79 and 80. Note that although *asaṅga* means non-attached, this is the negation of *saṅga* which has connotations and meanings similar to the term *Yoga*. It suggests a joining, a coming together, or a union. It also means touch or contact. Further it connotes friendliness, fondness and out-right attachment to worldly ties of various sorts.
3. *MK*. IV. 26 and 27.
4. *MK* III. 39 and IV. 2.
5. *MK* III. 37, 39, 40 and IV. 78.

the nature of consciousness, and in reference to philosophical disputation.[1]

Within the scope of these terms, Consciousness is a central issue especially in relation to the theory behind the practice of *sādhana*, and that of meditation or contemplation in particular. *Citta* has two meanings which differentiate the "empirical mind" and the "non-mind" or "unborn mind" of Pure Consciousness. In the first, the world is perceived as a result of the subject-object relationship, of the dual structure imposed by the workings of the mind. The mind is said to run after unreal objects due to attachment or the mental preoccupation with the dual world. However, the real nature of the mind or consciousness is that it is eternally unattached, never in touch with any object, and ever without relations. The mind "turns back" from duality to its pure condition when it becomes unattached. It is through the process of *Asparśa Yoga* that this condition of non-duality, of freedom and liberation, is realized. This is Gauḍapāda's soteriological purpose in the *Māṇḍūkya Kārikā.*

2. Summary of Gauḍapāda's Soteriological Purpose

Gauḍapāda is presented herein as an early preceptor in the established tradition of Advaita Vedānta. He is highly respected and revered within the tradition as both a philospher and religious teacher. Though his biography is unknown, the available hagiography describes him as a deeply religious individual, engrossed in meditation and other practices, who upon realization becomes a great and respected teacher to aspirants on the spiritual quest.

Gauḍapāda's work embodies his religious concern both philosophically and practically. His major text, the *Māṇḍūkya Kārikā*, is attached to and is a partial commentary on a scriptural text, the *Māṇḍūkyopaniṣad.* As an expository text of Vedāntic teachings, the *Kārikā* is referred to as an *upadeśa-śāstra* (instructional treatise). Its two-fold purpose is to teach the essentials of

1. Note the similar connection of the terms *asaṅga* and *asparśa* in the *Gītā.* See G II. 14, 48, V. 21, 22 and 23 in particular. This is briefly dealt with above in Chapter VI, section 5.

Advaita philosophy and set forth practical advice to help the *sādhaka* on the path of Self-realization.

There are certain stylistic elements of the text which further indicate the soteriological nature of Gauḍapāda's teachings as embodied in the *Kārikās*. First, Advaita Vedānta is found to be a *darśana* or system of thought which is a synthesis of philosophy and religion. As a *mokṣa* oriented system this involves the enquiry into the nature of reality and the search for the way to realize this knowledge. These two aspects are seen to be interrelated and mutually affect each other. Second, there is the theological concern of Advaita Vedānta and Gauḍapāda. The use of scripture as a valid source of knowledge, the exegesis and interpretation of *śruti*, and the continual references to traditional authorities suggest this religious orientation.

Third, Gauḍapāda's use of reason can be seen to have a religious or soteriological aspect. Philosophically it leads to right thinking and the understanding of the nature of reality. In this way it assists enquiry and aids the pursuit of realization. It helps to show the fallaciousness and erroneousness of the partial views concerning reality as well as enables the *sādhaka* to see the mutually contradictory nature of the multiple views concerning this. It poses problems or doubts and seeks rational solutions for them. Further, it allows intelligent use of scripture for this purpose and utilizes the basic method of reflection (*manana* and *vicāra*) to assist in the process of direct realization.

Gauḍapāda's epistemology places perception, reasoning, verbal testimony and revelation as mediate knowledge while he posits *jñāna* or *anubhūti* (intuition or direct experience) as the only truly valid means of knowledge (*pramāṇa*).

All this is aided in the *Māṇḍūkya Kārikā* by teaching devices such as explanations, arguments, examples, illustrations, figurative language and so forth. These are Gauḍapāda's means of expressing and communicating religious or spiritual experience. Also, in the text he combines a mastery of scripture, logical skill, and profound spiritual experience in his exposition of the theory and practice of *Brahma-vidyā*.

Gauḍapāda's metaphysics sketches the ideas of non-duality (*advaita*) and non-origination (*ajātivāda*) and indicates the nature of the world and of the individual from these perspectives. The soteriological context of the mokṣa or liberation orientation is found to be inherent within the metaphysics.

Gauḍapāda presents a phenomenology of experience and a unique meta-psychology. First he offers an analysis of the states of man's experience. This is followed by a discussion of his working psychology which includes an analysis of man as a psycho-physical being whose true nature is discovered as being spiritual. This also involves a study of the nature of the mind which is necessary to understand the place and importance of the meditative discipline advocated in Gauḍapāda's text. This psychological orientation has its metaphysical or philosophical side which, for example, can be seen in the explication of the ideas concerning "mind creation". Gauḍapāda discusses the problem of ignorance or spiritual sleep and its psychological causes as well as its correction through right knowledge which is further indicative of the soteriological aspect of his meta-psychology.

Chapters I through V deal with the above aspects and they provide the necessary background for Gauḍapāda's essential soteriological concern which is detailed in Chapter VI of this work. His soteriology concerns a specifically religious desire and activity. This is exhibited in the two-fold division of theory and that of actual practices undertaken in the pursuit of the perceived goal. These two supplement and mutually influence each other.

The first aspect is that of Gauḍapāda's conception of the religious or spiritual goal. This is his view of man's religious situation as being one of bondage and that *mokṣa* is the rightful end of man's existence. He states man's basic dissatisfaction with his life in the world and offers a description of this in contrast to the conception of salvation or liberation which he espouses. Cosmically, man participates in the bondange of *saṃsāra*, ignorant of the finitude and illusion of the manifold universe. Individually, man is said to suffer or feel a basic frustration and dissatisfaction with life, feeling a sense of alienation while living an essentially individualistic or separate existence from a basic egotistical orientation.

Gauḍapāda states that this is inauthentic living and that man's nature is really quite different. Rather than the cosmic condition of bondage there is complete freedom; the wheel of *saṃsāra* is really the unity of *Brahman*; the finitude, manifoldness and deceptiveness of phenomena is really the oneness of the totality of non-dual reality. Rather than living an alienated existence on an individual level, man is advised to partake of the peace and bliss of meaningful existence in perfect integration with the higher or deeper aspects of his being which are at one with the nature of plenary reality. The problem is that man is not aware of his true nature and does not have real knowledge of himself nor of the world in which he participates and exists. For this reason Gauḍapāda has to emphatically state this idea of liberation.

Mokṣa, then, is the *summum bonum* of life. Positively stated, it is the nature of freedom and independence, perfection, fullness and peace, supreme felicity and unexcellable bliss. It is the realization of the real Self (*ātman*) and the discovery of its oneness with, or non-difference from, Ultimate Reality (*Brahman*). Thus it is true knowledge (*jñāna*) or *Brahma-Vidyā*. From the perspective of this new affirmation, what was once seen as normal every-day living is severely depreciated and disvalued. In this way, *mokṣa* is negatively stated, as liberation, emancipation, release, or freedom from bondage, etc. It is an unbinding, un-fettering or un-burdening; a disencumbering or unattaching from delusory living. It can also be seen as a relief, rescue or delivery from suffering. Finally, in this light, it can be seen as final redemption, a reclaiming, recovery or restoring of authentic existence.

The second aspect of Gauḍapāda's soteriological concern is that of actual religio-spiritual practice. While first describing the situation of man and stating the need for positive transformation, he is also justifying the spiritual quest as a whole. This quest is not merely a theoretical one but a practical pursuit which consists of ways or methods to achieve liberation, to actualize this goal experientially. Gauḍapāda's *sādhanā* or spiritual discipline consists of the attitudes and techniques for spiritual unfoldment. He advocates the life of *sannyāsa* (renunciation), the development of the practices and virtues of *abhyāsa* (fixing the mind), *vairāgya* (dispassion), *viveka* (discrimination) and *vicāra* (self-enquiry). The main technique to be used is the *upāsanā* or meditation on the sacred syllable *OM*. Gauḍapāda proposes a progressive practice utilizing the different *mātrās* (syllables) of *AUM* until the *sādhaka* is practising the contemplation of the *mātrā*-less aspect. This is the final movement of the *ahaṅgraha upāsanā*, the turning inward towards the Self. It is the transformation of meditation into *nididhyāsana*, contemplation. This is the highest *jñāna Sādhanā* of traditional Vedānta, which Gauḍapāda calls *Asparśa Yoga*. The goal of this practice is the achievement of *nirvikalpa samādhi* wherein the mind attains the state of "non-mind" (*amanastā* or *amanībhāva*). When this occurs, knowledge (*jñāna*) becomes established in the Self, *Turīya* or *Brahman* is realized, and the condition of liberation accrues for the successful aspirant.

Once this *samādhi* is stabilized and the experience permeates the *sādhaka's* entire life, he truly becomes a *jñāni*, a "knower". As a Self-realized or a liberated man he experiences both himself and the world differently than before. For now he has attained the state of fearlessness (*abhayam padam*) which is free from sorrow and desire and duality is no longer perceived. Everything is the Self (*Ātman*) or *Brahman*. And his basically egotistical existence is transformed in conformity with this new understanding. Abiding thus he partakes of the peace and the bliss of true freedom. This is the dynamic spiritual condition of *jīvanmukti*, liberation while alive. The emancipated man participates in the world, though in a new way. Because his ego-hood has been subdued and replaced, as it were, by his true Self with which he is now identified, the world no longer touches him. He now experiences the world from a condition of perfect detachment (*asaṅga*). Thus this is a new mode of living—a living and doing without desire or attachment. It is the soteriological goal of Gauḍapāda's practical teachings.

In conclusion, Gauḍapāda's *Māṇḍūkya Kārikā* has been described, analyzed and interpreted in light of his soteriology. The religio-spiritual dimensions of his text have been presented in terms of its theoretical and practical levels. The integral unity of the various components of Gauḍapāda's system of thought is indicated. He is seen to synthesize philosophy and religion herein through his essential soteriological concern. Gauḍapāda is often only seen as a systematic philosopher to the relative neglect of his role as a religious teacher or preceptor. He and his text have thus been presented primarily from this latter religio-spiritual perspective. In this way Gauḍapāda's *Māṇḍūkya Kārikā* has been utilized as a concrete example and illustration of the tradition of Advaita Vedānta in an attempt to investigate the soteriology of this system.

BIBLIOGRAPHY

A. Translations of Texts and Commentaries

Māṇḍūkyopaniṣad, translation and notes by Swāmī Sarvānanda, with a summary of *Gauḍapāda's Kārikās* by Swāmī Tyāgīśānanda, Madras : Sri Ramakrishna Math, 1964.

Āgamaśāstra of Gauḍapāda, translated and annotated by Vidhushekhara Bhattacharya, University of Calcutta, 1943.

The Māṇḍūkyopaniṣad with Gauḍapāda's Kārikās and the Bhāṣya of Śaṅkara, translated into English by M. N. Dvivedi, The Bombay Theosophical Publication Fund, 1894.

Māṇḍūkya-Kārikās of Gauḍapāda, translated and annotated by R. D. Karmarkar, Government Oriental Series, Bhandarkar Oriental Research Institute, Poona, 1953.

Māṇḍūkyopaniṣad with Gauḍapāda's Kārikā and Śaṅkara's commentary, translated and annotated by Swāmī Nikhilānanda, Sri Ramakrishna Ashrama, Mysore, 1936.

Māṇḍūkya Upaniṣad and Kārikā, with Śaṅkara's commentary in Swāmī Gambhīrānanda, trans., *Eight Upaniṣads*, Vol. II, Calcutta : Advaita Ashrama, 1966, pp. 173-404.

B. Books and Articles Consulted

Agnihotri, B. S. "Influence of Yogopaniṣad on the Gauḍapāda Kārikās", *Proceedings of the All-India Oriental Conference* (1948), p. 126.

Bhattacharya, Haridas, (editor). *The Cultural Heritage of India*, 5 Vols., Calcutta : The Ramakrishna Mission Institute of Culture, 1953 (1937).

Bhattacharya, Vidhushekhara. *The Gauḍapāda-Kārikā on the* Māṇḍūkya Upanishad", *Proceedings of the All-India Oriental Conference*, No. 2 (1920-2), pp, 439-462.

Bhattacharya, Vidhushekhara, "Gauḍapāda", *Indian Historical Quarterly*, Vol. XIV (1938), pp. 392-397. (Also in the *Winternitz Memorial Volume*, Lahore 1940).

Bhattacharya, Vidhushekhara. "Asparśa-Yoga", in Mehar Chand Lachhman Das, *Woolner Commemorative Volume*, Lahore, 1940, pp. 19-20.

Bhattacharya, Vidhushekhara. "The Māṇḍūkya Upanishad and the Gauḍapāda Kārikā," *Indian Historical Quarterly*, Vol. I (1925), pp. 119-125, 295-302.

Brahma, Nalini Kanta. *Philosophy of Hindu Sādhana*, London : Kegan Paul, Trench, Trubner & Co., Ltd., 1932.

Chakraborty, N. B. "Gauḍapāda : his work and views", *Calcutta Review*, Vol. 145 (1957), pp. 89-96.

Chennakesavan, Sarasvati. *The Concept of Mind in Indian Philosophy*, Bombay : Asia Publishing House, 1960. Second Edition 1980 (MLBD) Delhi.

Conio, Caterina. *The Philosophy of the Māṇḍūkya Kārikā*, Varanasi: Bharatiya Vidya Prakasan, 1971.

Dasgupta, Surendranath. *A History of Indian Philosophy*, Vol. I, Cambridge : Cambridge University Press, 1922. Reprinted 1975 MLBD.

Dasgupta. *Indian Idealism*, Cambridge : Cambridge University Press, 1969, (1933).

Datta, D. M. *The Six Ways of Knowing*, Calcutta, University of Calcutta, 1960.

Deussen, Paul. *The Philosophy of the Upanishads*, New York : Dover Publications, Inc., 1966 (1906).

Deutsch, Eliot. *Advaita Vedānta : A Philosophical Reconstruction*, Honolulu : East-West Center Press, 1969.

Divanji, P. C., "Gauḍapāda's Asparśayoga and Śaṃkara's Jñānavāda", *Poona Orientalist*, Vol. 4 (1940), pp. 149-158.

Eliade, Mircea. *Yoga : Immortality and Freedom*, Princeton : Princeton University Press, second edition, 1969.

Farquhar, J. N. *An Outline of the Religious Literature of India*, Delhi : Motilal Banarsidass, 1967 (1920).

Guenon, Rene. *Man and His Becoming According to the Vedānta*, New York : Noonday Press, 1958.

Iyer, K. A. Krishnaswamy. *Vedānta or the Science of Reality*,

36. *Brahman* is birthless, sleepless, dreamless, nameless, formless, ever effulgent, everything, and a knower. (With regard to It) there is not the least possibility of ceremony.
37. The Self is free of all sense-organs, and is above all internal organs. It is supremely tranquil, eternal effulgence, divine absorption, immutable and fearless.
38. There can be no acceptance or rejection where all mentation stops. Then knowledge becomes established in the Self, and is unborn and poised in equality.
39. The *Yoga* that is familiarly referred to as without any touch with anything (*Asparśa Yoga*) is difficult to be comprehended by anyone of the *yogis*. For those *yogis*, who apprehend fear where there is no fear, are afraid of it.
40. For all these *yogis*, fearlessness, the removal of misery, knowledge (of the Self), and everlasting peace are dependent on the control of the mind.
41. Just as an ocean can be emptied with the help of the tip of a blade of *Kuśa* grass that can hold just a drop, so also can the control of the mind be brought about by absence of depression.
42. With the help of that proper process one should bring under discipline the mind that remains dispersed amidst objects of desire and enjoyment; and one should bring it under control even when it is in full peace in sleep, for sleep is as bad as desire.
43. Constantly remembering that everything is full of misery, one should withdraw the mind from the enjoyment arising out of desire. Remembering ever the fact that the birthless *Brahman* is everything, one does not surely perceive the born (viz. the host of duality).
44. One should wake up the mind merged in deep sleep; one should bring the dispersed mind into tranquillity again; one should know when the mind is tinged with desire (and is in a state of latency). One should not disturb the mind established in equipoise.
45. One should not enjoy happiness in that state; but one should become unattached through the use of discrimination. When the mind, established in steadiness, wants to issue out, one should concentrate it with diligence.

Mukhopadhyaya, Govindagopal. *Studies in the Upaniṣads*, Calcutta : Sanskrit College, 1960.

Nakamura, Hajime. "A Critical Survey of Indian Religion and Philosophy chiefly based upon Japanese Studies", *Acta Asiatica*, No. 5 (Tokyo 1963), pp. 1-75.

Potter, Karl H. "Attitudes, Games, and Indian Philosophy", *Philosophy East and West*, Vol. VI. 3 ((October, 1956), pp. 239-245.

Potter, Karl H. *Presuppositions of India's Philosophies*, Westport, Connecticut : Greewood press, 1972 (1963).

Prasad, Jwala. *History of Indian Epistemology*, Delhi : Munshiram Manoharlal, 1956.

Prithipal, D. *Advaita Vedānta*, Varanasi : Bharatiya Vidya Prakasan, 1969.

Radhakrishnan, S. *Indian Philosophy*, Vol. II, London : George Allen & Unwin, (2nd Ed.), 1929.

Raju, P. T. "The concept of the spiritual in Indian thought", *Philosophy East and West*, IV, 3 (Oct. 1954), pp. 195-214.

Raju, P. T. *Idealistic Thought of India*, Cambridge : Harvard University Press, 1953.

Raju, P. T. *The Philosophical Traditions af India*, London : George Allen & Unwin, 1971.

Raju, P. T. "An unnoticed aspect of Gauḍapāda's *Māṇḍūkya Kārikās*", *Annals of the Bhandarkar Oriental Research Institute*, Vol. 26, pp. 192-200.

Ranade, R. D. *A Constructive Survey of Upanishadic Philosophy*, Bombay, Bharatiya Vidya Bhavan, 1968.

Rao, K. B. Ramkrishna. *Three Lectures on Advaita as Philosophy and Religion*, Mysore, University of Mysore, 1969.

Reyna, Ruth. *The Concept of Māyā*, Bombay : Asia Publishing House, 1962.

Robinson, Richard H. "Classical Indian Philosophy", in Joseph W. Elder, ed. *Chapters in Indian Civilization*, Vol. I, Kendall Hunt Publishing Company, 1970.

Roy, B. A. Ṇ. "The *Māṇḍūkya Upaniṣad* and the *Kārikās* of Gauḍapāda", *Indian Historical Quarterly*, Vol. 14 (1938), pp. 564-9. Also found in *Winternitz Memorial Number*, pp. 364-9.

Roy, S. S. *The Heritage of Śaṅkara*, Allahabad: Udayana Publications, 1965.

Sahasrabudhe, M. T. *A Survey of the Pre-Śaṅkara Advaita Vedānta*, Poona : Poona University Press, 1968.

Saksena, Shri Krishna. *Essays on Indian Philosophy*, Honolulu : University of Hawaii Press, 1970.

Saksena, Shri Krishna. *Nature of Consciousness in Hindu Philosophy*, Delhi : Motilal Banarsidass, 1971 (1944).

Sarma, B. N. K. "Further Light on *Gauḍapāda-Kārikās*", *Review of Philosophy and Religion* (Poona), Vol. 3. 1, pp. 45-55.

Sarma, B. N. K. "New light on the *Gauḍapāda-Kārikās*", *Review of Philosophy and Religion* (Poona), Vol. 2. 1 (1931), pp. 35-56.

Sarma, B. N. K. "Still further light on the *Gauḍapāda-Kārikās*", *Review of Philosophy and Religion* (Poona), Vol. 4. 2, pp. 174-195.

Sarma, B. N. K. "Upanishadic theory of *Gauḍapāda's Kārikās*", *Poona Orientalist*, Vol. 1. 2 (1936-7), pp. 27-38.

Sarma, Y. Subrahmanya. *Avasthatraya or the Unique Method of Vedanta*, Bangalore : Adhyatma Prakasha Karyalaya, 1937.

Sarma, Y. Subrahmanya. "The Upanishadic theory of the *Gauḍapāda-kārikās*", *Review of Philosophy and Religion* (Poona), Vol. 4. 2 (1933), pp. 196-204.

Sastri, S. S. "Some observations on the *Māṇḍūkya-Kārikās*", *Journal of Oriental Research* (Madras), Vol. 3 (1939).

Sharma, Chandradhar. *A Critical Survey af Indian Philosophy*, Delhi : Motilal Banarsidass, 1964 (1960).

Sinari, Ramakant A. *The Structure of Indian Thought*, Springfield, Illinois : Charles C. Thomas, 1970.

Sinha, Jadunath. *A History of Indian Philosophy*, Vol. II, Calcutta: Central Book Agency, 1952.

Sinha, Jadunath. *Indian Epistemology of Perception*, Calcutta, Sinha Publishing House Private Ltd., 1969.

Smart, Ninian. *Doctrine and Argument in Indian Philosophy*, London: George Allen & Unwin Ltd., 1964.

Solomon, E. A. *Avidyā—A Problem of Truth and Reality*, Ahmedabad : Gujarat University, 1969.

Streng, Frederick, J. *Emptiness : A Study in Religious Meaning*, Nashville : Abingdon Press, 1967.

Subbiah, A. V. "Gauḍapāda's *Āgamaśāstra*", *Indian Historical Quarterly*, Vol. 11 (1935), pp. 783-790.

Subbiah, A. V. "The *Māṇḍūkyopaniṣad* and Gauḍapāda", *Indian Antiquary*, Vol. 62 (1933), pp. 181-193.

Sundaram, P. K. *Advaita Epistemology*, Madras : University of Madras, 1968.

Swāmī Agehānanda Bhāratī. *A Functional Analysis of Indian Thought and its Social Margins*, Varanasi : Chowkhamba Sanskrit Series Office, 1964.

Swāmī Bhoomananda Tirtha. *Brahma Vidya Abhyasa*, Vol. I, Trichur Kerala : Narayanasrama Thapovanam, 1968.

Swāmī Bhoomananda Tirtha. *Brahma Vidya Abhyasa*, Vol. II, Trichur Kerala : Narayanasrama Thapovanam, 1970.

Swāmī Chinmayananda. *Discourses on Mandukya Upanishad with Gauḍapāda's Karika*, Madras : Chinmaya Publication Trust, 1953.

Swāmī Iswarananda. *God-Realization Through Reason*, Trichur Kerala : Sri Ramakrishna Ashrama, 1959.

Swāmī Madhavananda, trans. *The Bṛhadāraṇyaka Upaniṣad*, Calcutta : Advaita Ashrama, fourth edition, 1965.

Swāmī Poornananda Tirtha. *Brahma Vidya*, Wadakancheri Kerala : Jnana Asram, 1966.

Swāmī Purushottama Tirtha. "*The thre estates analysed*", *Kaivalya Sudha*, Vol. 8, No. 11 (15 November, 1971), pp. 3-13.

Swāmī Rāmānanda Tīrtha. *A Writer's Study of Śaṅkara versus the Six Preceptors of Advaita*, Madras : Tinniyam Śaṅkara Mutt Bhakta Jana Sabha, 1970.

Swāmī Satchidanandendra Saraswati. *Salient Features of Śaṅkara's Vedānta*, Holenarsipur : Adhyatma Prakasha Karyalaya, 1967.

Warrier, A. G. Krishna. *The Concept of Mukti in Advaita Vedānta*, Madras : University of Madras, 1961.

Warrier, A. G. Krishna. "Gauḍapāda and Śaṃkara (a study in contrast)", *Annals of the Bhandarkar Oriental Research Institute* (Poona) 48/49 (1968), pp. 179-186.

Appendix I

THE PRINCIPAL UPADEŚA SECTION OF GAUḌAPĀDA'S *MĀṆḌŪKYA KĀRIKĀ*

MK III

29. As in dream the mind vibrates, as though having dual aspects, so in the waking state the mind vibrates as though with two facets.
30. There is no doubt that in dream, the mind, though one, appears in dual aspects; so also in the waking state, the mind, though one, appears to have two aspects.
31. All this that there is—together with all that moves or does not move—is perceived by the mind (and therefore all this is but the mind); for when the mind ceases to be the mind, duality is no longer perceived.
32. When, following the instruction of scriptures and the teacher, the mind ceases to think as a consequence of the realisation of the Truth that is the Self, then the mind attains the state of not being the mind; in the absence of things to be perceived, it becomes a non-perceiver.
33. They say that the non-conceptual knowledge, that is birthless, is non-different from the knowable (*Brahman*). The knowledge that has *Brahman* for its content is birthless and everlasting. The birthless (Self) is known by the birthless (knowledge).
34. The behaviour that the mind has, when it is under control, free from all ideation, and full of discrimination, should be particularly noted. The behaviour of the mind in deep sleep is different and is not similar to that (of the controlled mind).
35. For that mind loses itself in sleep, but does not lose itself when under control. That very mind becomes the fearless *Brahman*, possessed of the light of Consciousness all around.

INDEX